Special Needs Workbook

HOLT, RINEHART AND WINSTON
A Harcourt Education Company
Orlando • **Austin** • New York • San Diego • Toronto • London

TO THE TEACHER

Help students that have individual needs succeed and master the content in the text with this *Special Needs Workbook*. This booklet contains modified Directed Reading worksheets and modified Chapter Tests to ensure that your whole class is learning the same content. The questions are simplified and contain lower level vocabulary, but content accuracy is maintained. The booklet is designed to help students navigate the questions easily. And the booklet includes multiple-choice, fill in the blank, matching, and interpreting graphics questions.

Printed in the United States of America

ISBN 0-03-036053-6
3 4 5   862   09 08 07 06 05

Contents

Name ______________________ Class ______________ Date ______________

Skills Worksheet

Directed Reading B

Section: Asking About Life

Circle the letter of the best answer for each question.

1. What is the study of living things called?

a. technology

b. life science

c. investigation

d. asking questions

IT ALL STARTS WITH A QUESTION

2. What do algae, redwood trees, and whales show?

a. the diversity of life

b. life science

c. lab investigations

d. asking questions

In Your Own Backyard

3. Which of the following is a life science question you might ask about an organism?

a. Can that model airplane fly?

b. What is your dog's name?

c. How are you feeling today?

d. Why do leaves change color in the fall?

LIFE SCIENTISTS

Anyone

Circle the letter of the best answer for each question.

4. Who can become a life scientist?

a. only men

b. only women

c. only people who can see

d. anyone who wants to

Anywhere

5. Life scientists can work

a. only in a laboratory.

b. mostly in hospitals.

c. anywhere they can study living things.

d. only where there are trees.

Anything

6. What decides what a life scientist studies?

a. where the person lives

b. what interests the person

c. being a man or woman

d. the time of year

WHY ASK QUESTIONS?

Read the words in the box. Read the sentences. Fill in each blank with the words or phrase that best completes the sentence.

diseases	tigers	inherited

Fighting Diseases

7. Life scientists learn about ______________________ in order to try to find cures.

Understanding Inherited Diseases

8. Cystic fibrosis is one of many ______________________ diseases.

Protecting the Environment

9. One life scientist helps the environment by studying Siberian ______________________.

Name ______________________ Class ______________ Date ____________

Skills Worksheet

Directed Reading B

Section: Scientific Methods

WHAT ARE SCIENTIFIC METHODS?

Read the words in the box. Read the sentences. Fill in each blank with the words or phrase that best completes the sentence.

counting	asking questions
accurate	scientific methods

1. The ______________________ are a series of steps scientists use to solve problems.

2. One step of the scientific methods is ______________________.

ASK A QUESTION

Make Observations

3. The students made observations by ______________________ deformed frogs.

Accurate Observations

4. Observations are useful only if they are ______________________.

FORM A HYPOTHESIS

Read the words in the box. Read the sentences. Fill in each blank with the words or phrase that best completes the sentence.

hypothesis	if – then

5. A possible answer to a question is a(n) ______________________________.

Predictions

6. A prediction is a(n) ______________________________ statement.

TEST THE HYPOTHESIS

controlled experiment	variable	factor

7. Anything in an experiment that can influence an experiment's outcome is considered a ______________________________.

Under Control

8. An experiment that tests only one factor at a time is a ______________________________.

9. The factor that differs between groups in an experiment is the ______________________________.

Designing an Experiment

Circle the letter of the best answer for each question.

10. What does designing an experiment require?

a. planning

b. factors

c. many variables

d. light

Collecting Data

11. Why do scientists try to test many plants or animals?

a. to be more certain of their data

b. to get a good hypothesis

c. to have many variables

d. to have a big experiment

ANALYZE THE RESULTS

12. What do scientists do before they analyze the results of an experiment?

a. They organize the data.

b. They begin a new experiment.

c. They draw a conclusion.

d. They write up their results.

DRAW CONCLUSIONS

13. What are scientists deciding when they draw conclusions?

a. whether to put the data in a graph

b. which factor is the variable

c. whether the results support a hypothesis

d. which group should be the control group

Is It the Answer?

<u>Circle the letter</u> of the best answer for each question.

14. What is true about finding an answer to a question?

a. It may begin another investigation.

b. No more questions can arise.

c. The question was not good.

d. The experiment was done wrong.

COMMUNICATE RESULTS

15. What do scientists usually do with their results?

a. sell them

b. share them

c. put them away

d. destroy them

Name ______________________________ Class ______________ Date ____________

Skills Worksheet

Directed Reading B

Section: Scientific Models

TYPES OF SCIENTIFIC MODELS

Circle the letter of the best answer for each question.

1. What is a representation of an object or system?

a. a model

b. a prediction

c. an observation

d. a limitation

2. What is a problem with models?

a. They are small.

b. They are not real.

c. They are on computers.

d. They may be physical.

3. Which of these is NOT a type of scientific model?

a. fashion model

b. conceptual model

c. mathematical model

d. physical model

Physical Models

4. Which is a physical model?

a. an equation

b. a comparison

c. a toy rocket

d. human bones

Mathematical Models

Circle the letter of the best answer for each question.

5. What kind of model is made of numbers and equations?

a. mathematical model

b. scientific method

c. physical model

d. conceptual model

6. What do scientists use the Punnett square to predict?

a. how traits are passed to offspring

b. when traits appear in parents

c. which mathematical model to use

d. how complex a model is

Conceptual Models

7. What kind of scientific model is based on systems of ideas?

a. mathematical model

b. physical model

c. computer model

d. conceptual model

BENEFITS OF MODELS

8. What kinds of things are models used to show?

a. common things

b. things that no longer exist

c. very simple things

d. things of average size

BUILDING SCIENTIFIC KNOWLEDGE

Scientific Theories

Circle the letter of the best answer for each question.

9. What is an explanation that unites a broad range of facts?

a. an idea

b. a theory

c. an hypothesis

d. a law

Scientific Laws

10. What kind of scientific idea rarely changes?

a. an idea

b. a theory

c. an hypothesis

d. a law

Scientific Change

11. Which of the following is true of scientific facts or laws?

a. Many started as hypotheses.

b. They never are contradicted.

c. They are the same thing as theories.

d. They are conceptual models.

Name ______________________ Class ______________ Date ______________

Skills Worksheet

Directed Reading B

Section: Tools, Measurement, and Safety

Read the words in the box. Read the sentences. Fill in each blank with the words or phrase that best completes the sentence.

technology	analyze data
tools	computer

1. Life scientists use various ______________________ to help them with their work.

COMPUTERS AND TECHNOLOGY

2. The use of machines to meet human needs is called ______________________.

3. The first ______________________ was built in 1946.

4. Scientists use computers to ______________________.

TOOLS FOR SEEING

Read the description. Then draw a line from the dot to the matching word.

5. passes electrons through something to make a 3-D image •
6. passes electrons through something to make a flat image •
7. is made up of three main parts: a tube with lenses, a stage, and a light •
8. sends electromagnetic waves through the body to make images •

a. magnetic resonance imaging

b. scanning electron microscope

c. compound light microscope

d. transmission electron microscope

MEASUREMENT

Circle the letter of the best answer for each question.

9. Which is an advantage of the SI system?

a. is based on grains of wheat

b. it helps scientists share information

c. is based on astronomy

d. it works most of the time

Length

10. Which unit is used for measuring length?

a. grams (g)

b. milliliters (mL)

c. millimeters (mm)

d. cubic centimeters (cm^3)

Area

11. What is a measure of how much surface an object has?

a. area

b. length

c. micrometers

d. volume

Volume

12. Which of the following is NOT used to measure volume?

a. square micrometer

b. cubic centimeter

c. milliliter

d. liter

Circle the letter of the best answer for each question.

13. What term refers to the amount of space an object takes up?

a. its length

b. its area

c. its volume

d. its mass

Mass

14. What term refers to the amount of matter in an object?

a. its length

b. its area

c. its volume

d. its mass

Temperature

15. Which units are part of the International System of Units?

a. kelvins

b. ounces

c. degrees Fahrenheit

d. degrees

16. What shows how much energy is in matter?

a. its mass

b. its temperature

c. its volume

d. its length

SAFETY RULES!

Read the description. Then, draw a line from the dot next to each description to the matching picture.

17. hand safety ● **a.**

18. eye protection ● **b.**

19. plant safety ● **c.**

20. electric safety ● **d.**

Name ______________________ Class ______________ Date ____________

Assessment

Chapter Test C

The World of Life Science

MULTIPLE CHOICE

Circle the letter of the best answer for each question.

1. Which work might a life scientist do?

a. Build robots.

b. Study Siberian tigers.

c. Study what affects flooding.

d. Research comets in space.

2. Which tool has a tube with lenses, a stage, and a light?

a. a scanning electron microscope

b. a compound light microscope

c. a transmission electron microscope

d. an MRI

3. Which units are part of the International System of Units?

a. inches

b. milliliter

c. pounds

d. degrees Fahrenheit

4. Which of these is NOT a type of scientific model?

a. mathematical model

b. physical model

c. fashion model

d. conceptual model

MULTIPLE CHOICE

Circle the letter of the best answer for each question.

5. Which is a step of the scientific methods?

a. asking questions

b. stating a theory

c. using technology

d. building a microscope

6. Which of the following differs between groups in a controlled experiment?

a. a test

b. a prediction

c. a variable

d. a hypothesis

7. Which is a physical model?

a. a comparison

b. an equation

c. a toy airplane

d. a graph

8. What term refers to the amount of space an object takes up?

a. volume

b. mass

c. area

d. length

9. Which describes a compound light microscope?

a. It passes electrons through something to make a 3-D image.

b. It passes electrons through something to make a flat image.

c. It sends electromagnetic waves through the body to make images.

d. It is made up of three main parts: a tube with lenses, a stage, and a light.

MATCHING

Read the description. Then, draw a line from the dot next to each description to the matching word.

10. a possible explanation for observations ●

11. the amount of space something occupies ●

12. the amount of matter in an object ●

13. an explanation that unites a broad range of facts ●

a. volume

b. hypothesis

c. mass

d. theory

---

14. the use of machines to meet human needs ●

15. the study of living things ●

16. a series of steps followed by scientists to solve problems ●

17. a kind of scientific idea that rarely changes ●

a. life science

b. technology

c. scientific methods

d. law

FILL-IN-THE-BLANK

Read the words in the box. Read the sentences. Fill in each blank with the word or phrase that best completes the sentence.

model	scientific methods
life science	controlled experiment

18. A ______________________ is a representation of an object or a system.

19. The steps scientists use to answer questions are called ______________________.

20. A ______________________ tests only one factor at a time.

21. The study of living things is ______________________.

Name ______________________________ Class ________________ Date ______________

Skills Worksheet

Directed Reading B

Section: Characteristics of Living Things

Circle the letter of the best answer for each question.

1. How many characteristics do all living things share?

a. 1

b. 5

c. 6

d. 10

LIVING THINGS HAVE CELLS

2. What is one characteristic that all living things share?

a. They have eyes.

b. They have cells.

c. They have hair.

d. They have skin.

3. How many cells do all living things have?

a. 0

b. only 1

c. 1 or more

d. more than 100

4. What has all the materials necessary for life?

a. a cell

b. air

c. water

d. a membrane

Circle the letter of the best answer for each question.

5. What keeps a cell's contents away from its environment?

a. an outer husk

b. a watery cushion

c. a hard shell

d. a membrane

LIVING THINGS SENSE AND RESPOND TO CHANGE

6. What are all living things able to do?

a. They can sense and respond to change.

b. They can smell.

c. They can taste.

d. They can see.

Read the words in the box. Read the sentences. Fill in each blank with the word or phrase that best completes the sentence.

homeostasis	stable
stimulus	shiver

7. A change that affects a living thing's activity is a(n) ______________________.

Homeostasis

8. All living things must maintain a(n) ______________________ internal condition.

9. The maintenance of a stable internal condition is called ______________________.

Responding to External Changes

10. People ______________________ in order to warm up their bodies.

LIVING THINGS REPRODUCE

Read the words in the box. Read the sentences. Fill in each blank with the word or phrase that best completes the sentence.

asexual	reproduce
single-celled	sexual

11. One characteristic that all living things share is that they can ______________________.

12. Two parents produce offspring through ______________________ reproduction.

13. A single parent produces offspring through ______________________ reproduction.

14. Most ______________________ living things reproduce through asexual reproduction.

LIVING THINGS HAVE DNA

DNA	heredity
offspring	cells

15. The cells of all living things contain ______________________.

16. DNA, or deoxyribonucleic acid, controls the structure and function of ______________________.

17. When living things reproduce, they pass copies of their DNA to their ______________________.

18. The passing of traits from parents to offspring is called ______________________.

LIVING THINGS USE ENERGY

Circle the letter of the best answer for each question.

19. Which of the following is NOT an activity of life?

a. breaking down food

b. building cells

c. making food

d. changing liquids to gas

20. What is the total of all chemical activities a living thing performs called?

a. homeostasis

b. heredity

c. metabolism

d. stimulus

LIVING THINGS GROW AND DEVELOP

21. What do all living things do during their lives?

a. They grow and develop.

b. They shrink.

c. They stay the same.

d. They go through five stages.

22. What happens to a single-celled living thing as it grows?

a. It gets larger and divides.

b. It gains cells and gets bigger.

c. It gets larger, then explodes.

d. It gains cells but stays the same size.

23. What happens to a living thing with many cells as it grows?

a. It gets larger and divides.

b. It gains cells and gets bigger.

c. It gets larger, then explodes.

d. It gains cells but stays the same size.

Name ____________________ Class ____________ Date ____________

Skills Worksheet

Directed Reading B

Section: The Necessities of Life

Circle the letter of the best answer for each question.

WATER

1. What is the human body mostly made of?

a. air

b. fat

c. skin

d. water

2. How much of the cells of most living things is water?

a. about 5%

b. about 50%

c. about 70%

d. about 99%

3. How many days can a person survive without water?

a. about 1

b. about 3

c. about 7

d. about 10

AIR

4. What are two gases in air?

a. oxygen and carbon dioxide

b. oxygen and carbon monoxide

c. oxygen and sulfur dioxide

d. oxygen and nitrogen dioxide

Circle the letter of the best answer for each question.

5. What do most living things use to release energy from food?

a. carbon dioxide

b. oxygen

c. water

d. oxygen and carbon dioxide

6. What do green plants need to release energy from food?

a. carbon dioxide

b. oxygen

c. water

d. oxygen and carbon dioxide

A PLACE TO LIVE

7. What do all living things need where they live?

a. the ocean

b. tall trees

c. nitrogen and carbon monoxide

d. all things needed to survive

FOOD

8. What do living things use from food to replace cells and build body parts?

a. energy

b. nutrients

c. water

d. cells

Making Food

Read the words in the box. Read the sentences. Fill in each blank with the word or phrase that best completes the sentence.

consumers	frog	producers
decomposers	mushroom	plant

9. Living things that can make their own food

are ______________________.

10. A living thing that is a producer is

a(n) ______________________.

Taking Food

11. Living things that eat other organisms to get food

are ______________________.

12. A living thing that is a consumer is

a(n) ______________________.

13. Living things that get food by breaking down nutrients of dead

living things are ______________________.

14. A living thing that is a decomposer is

a(n) ______________________.

PUTTING IT ALL TOGETHER

Read the words in the box. Read the sentences. Fill in each blank with the word or phrase that best completes the sentence.

proteins	nutrients	molecule
amino acids	enzyme	hemoglobin

15. All living things break down food to use the ________________ in it.

16. The substance made when two or more atoms combine is called a(n) ________________.

PROTEINS

Making Proteins

17. Almost all of a cell's life processes involve ________________.

18. Proteins are large molecules made of smaller molecules called ________________.

Proteins in Action

19. A protein in red blood cells that binds to oxygen is ________________.

20. A protein that speeds up chemical reactions in cells is a(n) ________________.

CARBOHYDRATES

Read the words in the box. Read the sentences. Fill in each blank with the word or phrase that best completes the sentence.

simple	energy	fruits
complex	carbohydrate	starch

21. A molecule made of sugar is a(n) ______________________.

22. Carbohydrates are a source of ______________________ for cells.

Simple Carbohydrates

23. One sugar molecule or a few linked sugar molecules make up ______________________ carbohydrates.

24. Two examples of simple carbohydrates are table sugar and sugar in ______________________.

Complex Carbohydrates

25. Living things store extra sugar as ______________________ carbohydrates, which are made of hundreds of sugar molecules.

26. Plants, such as potatoes, store extra sugar as ______________________.

LIPIDS

Circle the letter of the best answer for each question.

27. What is a compound that cannot mix with water?

a. ATP

b. nucleic acid

c. lipid

d. carbohydrate

Phospholipids

28. What molecules form much of the cell membrane?

a. hemoglobin

b. phospholipids

c. enzymes

d. ATP

Fats and Oils

29. What are two lipids that store energy?

a. fats and oils

b. phospholipids and oils

c. starches and oils

d. starches and fats

ATP

30. What molecule carries most of the energy in the cell?

a. carbohydrate

b. lipid

c. ATP

d. nucleic acid

Circle the letter of the best answer for each question.

31. What two molecules transfer their energy to ATP to provide fuel for cells?

a. carbohydrates and lipids

b. enzymes and nucleic acids

c. amino acids and nucleic acids

d. amino acids and lipids

NUCLEIC ACIDS

32. What molecules are sometimes called the blueprints of life?

a. carbohydrates

b. lipids

c. ATP

d. nucleic acids

33. What type of molecule is DNA?

a. a carbohydrate

b. a lipid

c. ATP

d. a nucleic acid

Name ______________________ Class ______________ Date ____________

Assessment

Chapter Test C

It's Alive!! Or Is It?

MULTIPLE CHOICE

Circle the letter of the best answer for each question.

1. What are all living things made of?

a. one cell

b. one or more cells

c. several hundred cells

d. trillions of cells

2. What are food, water, air, and a place to live?

a. characteristics of living things

b. basic needs of most living things

c. examples of living things

d. stimuli

3. How much of the human body is water?

a. about 10%

b. about 50%

c. about 70%

d. about 99%

4. What are hunger, sounds, and light?

a. examples of stimuli

b. characteristics of life

c. necessities of life

d. experiences all living things share

MULTIPLE CHOICE

Circle the letter of the best answer for each question.

5. What is DNA?

a. a carbohydrate

b. a protein

c. a lipid

d. a nucleic acid

6. What is one thing all living things do?

a. They grow and develop.

b. They stay the same.

c. They shrink as they get older.

d. They go through five stages.

7. What is one characteristic that all living things share?

a. Their cells have DNA.

b. They can smell and taste.

c. They can move.

d. They have two or more cells.

8. How do people warm up their bodies when they are cold?

a. sweat

b. shiver

c. move to a shady area

d. stay still

9. What is the passing of traits from parent to offspring called?

a. sexual reproduction

b. homeostasis

c. heredity

d. DNA

MATCHING

Read the description. Then, <u>draw a line</u> from the dot next to each description to the matching word.

10. the maintenance of a stable internal condition ●

11. the sum of all chemical activities a living thing performs ●

12. molecule that forms much of the cell membrane ●

13. molecule that is the major energy carrier in the cell ●

a. metabolism

b. phospholipid

c. ATP

d. homeostasis

---

14. molecule made up of amino acids ●

15. molecule made of sugar ●

16. molecule sometimes called the blueprints of life ●

17. fats and oils ●

a. protein

b. lipids

c. carbohydrate

d. nucleic acid

FILL-IN-THE-BLANK

Read the words in the box. Read the sentences. Fill in each blank with the word or phrase that best completes the sentence.

producer	decomposer
asexual	consumer

18. A single-celled living thing reproduces through

______________________ reproduction.

19. A living thing that makes its own food is

a(n) ______________________.

20. A living thing that eats other organisms is

a(n) ______________________.

21. A living thing that breaks down the nutrients of dead organisms

is a(n) ______________________.

Name ______________________ Class ______________ Date ____________

Skills Worksheet

Directed Reading B

Section: The Diversity of Cells

Circle the letter of the best answer for each question.

1. Which phrase contains the most important fact about cells?

a. discovered with microscopes

b. are basic units of life

c. are too small to see

d. discovered by accident

CELLS AND CELL THEORY

Read the words in the box. Read the sentences. Fill in each blank with the word that best completes the sentence.

animals	cells	microscope	plants

2. Robert Hooke was the first person to describe

______________________________.

3. Hooke built a(n) ______________________________ and used it to look at cells.

4. Hooke spent most of his time looking at the cells

of ______________________________.

5. Hooke's microscope could not see the cells

of ______________________________.

Finding Cells in Other Organisms

Circle the letter of the best answer for each question.

6. Where did Leeuwenhoek find what he called *animalcules*?

a. in animal blood

b. in bread dough

c. in cells

d. in pond scum

The Cell Theory

7. Which of these is not a part of the cell theory?

a. Most cells are too small to be seen without a microscope.

b. All organisms are made of one or more cells

c. The cell is the basic unit of all living things.

d. All cells come from existing cells.

CELL SIZE

A Few Large Cells

8. Why can a chicken egg grow so large?

a. It is a single cell.

b. It has a yolk and a shell.

c. It does not have to take in food.

d. It grows faster than small cells.

Many Small Cells

9. What limits most cells to a very small size?

a. the surface area–to-volume ratio

b. the size of the nucleus

c. the amount of fluid in the cell

d. the hardness of the cell wall

PARTS OF A CELL

The Cell Membrane and Cytoplasm

Read the words in the box. Read the sentences. Fill in each blank with the word or phrase that best completes the sentence.

cells	cytoplasm	cell membrane

10. The layer that protects a cell from its environment is the ______________________.

11. The fluid inside a cell is called ______________________.

12. The cell membrane and cytoplasm are two parts of all ______________________.

Organelles

Circle the letter of the best answer for each question.

13. Which sentence is true about most organelles?

a. They float outside the cell.
b. They have specific functions in the cell.
c. They live in green algae.
d. They are always the same.

Genetic Material

14. What is the organelle which contains the cell's DNA called?

a. membrane
b. nucleus
c. cell wall
d. cytoplasm

TWO KINDS OF CELLS

Read the words in the box. Read the sentences. Fill in each blank with the word or phrase that best completes the sentence.

cells	eukaryotic	prokaryotic

15. The two groups of ______________________ are eukaryotic and prokaryotic.

16. Cells that are ______________________ have a nucleus.

17. Cells that are ______________________ do not have a nucleus.

PROKARYOTES: EUBACTERIA AND ARCHAEBACTERIA

Eubacteria

Circle the letter of the best answer for each question.

18. What is the common name for eubacteria?

a. prokaryote
b. ribosome
c. bacteria
d. flagellum

Archaebacteria

19. What is one way in which archaebacteria differ from eubacteria?

a. Archaebacteria lack of a nucleus.
b. Archaebacteria have a cell membrane.
c. Archaebacteria are single-celled.
d. Archaebacterial ribosomes are different.

Circle the letter of the best answer for each question.

20. Which group includes extremophiles?

a. eubacteria

b. archaebacteria

c. methane gases

d. eukaryotes

EUKARYOTIC CELLS AND EUKARYOTES

21. What does a eukaryote have that a prokaryote does not?

a. one or more cells

b. cells with a nucleus

c. cells with DNA

d. cells with membranes

22. Which of these words describes you and other humans?

a. eukaryote

b. prokaryote

c. protist

d. fungus

Name ______________________ Class ______________ Date ____________

Skills Worksheet

Directed Reading B

Section: Eukaryotic Cells

CELL WALL

Circle the letter of the best answer for each question.

1. What is the purpose of a cell wall?

a. to make a plant droop

b. to support the cell

c. to carry DNA

d. to digest cellulose

CELL MEMBRANE

2. What is the purpose of a cell membrane?

a. to make lipids

b. to make phospholipids

c. to protect the cell

d. to support the cell wall

3. What does having two layers allow the cell membrane to do?

a. make lipids and phospholipids

b. support the cell wall

c. make proteins

d. pass nutrients and wastes through

CYTOSKELETON

4. What is the cytoskeleton made of?

a. cells

b. lipids

c. membranes

d. proteins

Circle the letter of the best answer for each question.

5. What is the cytoskeleton's job in the cell?

a. help keep the cell's shape

b. process proteins

c. store water

d. produce energy

NUCLEUS

6. What is the genetic material inside a cell's nucleus?

a. protein

b. lipids

c. DNA

d. nucleolis

7. What is the function of proteins in a cell?

a. to control chemical reactions

b. to store genetic information

c. to cover the nucleus

d. to copy messages from DNA

8. What is an amino acid?

a. part of the cell membrane

b. another term for DNA

c. a dangerous chemical

d. a molecule used to make proteins

RIBOSOMES

Circle the letter of the best answer for each question.

9. What do all ribosomes do?

a. make proteins

b. float in the cytoplasm

c. attach themselves to membranes

d. make organelles

ENDOPLASMIC RETICULUM

10. What does the endoplasmic reticulum look like?

a. oval, with pores

b. small and round

c. long, with many folds

d. a bubble full of liquid

11. Which phrase tells the function of the endoplasmic reticulum?

a. internal delivery system

b. protein factory

c. DNA storage

d. web of proteins

MITOCHONDRIA

Circle the letter of the best answer for each question.

12. What are the peanut-shaped organelles that break down sugar?

a. Golgi complex

b. cell membranes

c. ribosomes

d. mitochondria

CHLOROPLASTS

13. Which process happens inside a chloroplast?

a. making ATP

b. making DNA

c. photosynthesis

d. formation of animal cells

GOLGI COMPLEX

14. What long, folded cell part serves to package and distribute proteins?

a. Golgi complex

b. cell membrane

c. ribosome

d. cytoplasm

CELL COMPARTMENTS

15. Why do vesicles move around the cytoplasm?

a. to make new proteins

b. to move material around

c. to support the cell membrane

d. to form the Golgi complex

CELLULAR DIGESTION

Circle the letter of the best answer for each question.

16. What do lysosomes do?

a. make new proteins

b. move material around

c. get rid of waste and digest food

d. create vesicles

Vacuoles

17. What is a function of some vacuoles?

a. to make proteins

b. to store water

c. to make sugar

d. to harden the cell

ORGANELLES AND THEIR FUNCTIONS

The Cell Membrane and Cytoplasm

Read the words in the box. Read the sentences. Fill in each blank with the word or phrase that best completes the sentence.

chloroplasts	endoplasmic reticulum	lysosomes
mitochondria	nucleus	

18. The cell part that contains most of the DNA is

the ______________________________.

19. The part that makes lipids and breaks down drugs is

the ______________________________.

20. Cell parts that break down molecules to make ATP are

called ______________________________.

21. Plant cell parts that use the sun to make food are

called ______________________________.

22. Vesicles that break down food particles and cellular wastes

are called ______________________________.

Name ______________________ Class ______________ Date ______________

Skills Worksheet

Directed Reading B

Section: The Organization of Living Things

THE BENEFITS OF BEING MULTICELLULAR

Circle the letter of the best answer for each question.

1. Which of these is a benefit of being a large organism?

a. cell specialization

b. larger cells

c. smaller cells

d. shorter lifespan

CELLS WORKING TOGETHER

2. What is a *tissue* made of?

a. cells that work together

b. larger than normal cells

c. cells with longer lives

d. cardiac muscle

3. What organisms have nerve, muscle, connective, and protective tissues?

a. animals

b. plants

c. fungi

d. cardiac muscles

TISSUES WORKING TOGETHER

4. What is made up of two or more tissues working together?

a. a cell

b. a connective tissue

c. an organ

d. a group of specialized cells

5. Which of these is a plant organ?

a. heart

b. leaf

c. blood

d. transport tissue

ORGANS WORKING TOGETHER

Circle the letter of the best answer for each question.

6. What do you call a group of organs that work together to perform a particular function?

a. connective organs
b. an organism
c. an organ system
d. a human being

ORGANISMS

7. What is the term for anything that can perform a life process?

a. a cell
b. an organ system
c. an organization
d. an organism

8. Which of these is the lowest level of organization?

a. cells
b. tissues
c. organs
d. organ systems

STRUCTURE AND FUNCTION

9. What is the word for the arrangement of parts in an organism?

a. function
b. structure
c. cell
d. shape

10. What is a part's structure related to?

a. its function
b. its material
c. support from its cells
d. its ability to get rid of wastes

Assessment

Chapter Test C

Cells: The Basic Units of Life

MULTIPLE CHOICE

Circle the letter of the best answer for each question.

1. Which phrase describes a cell?

a. is always very small

b. does everything needed for life

c. always looks like an egg

d. is found only in plants

2. What are all organisms made of?

a. plants

b. protists

c. cells

d. eggs

3. Where do all cells come from?

a. animals

b. ponds

c. cells

d. eggs

4. What keeps the size of most cells very small?

a. their hard shells

b. the surface area–to-volume ratio

c. food and wastes

d. their thin surfaces

5. What protects the inside of a cell from the outside world?

a. cytoplasm

b. nucleus

c. cell membrane

d. DNA

Circle the letter of the best answer for each question.

6. How are archaebacteria different from eubacteria?

a. Archaebacteria have different ribosomes.

b. Archaebacteria have only one cell.

c. Archaebacteria have cell membranes.

d. Archaebacteria have RNA, not DNA.

7. What is cytoplasm?

a. the nucleus of a cell

b. the fluid inside a cell

c. the genetic material in a cell

d. the proteins in a cell

8. Where does photosynthesis take place in a cell?

a. in the nucleus

b. in the mitochondria

c. in the chloraplasts

d. in the ribosomes

9. What does the Golgi complex do in a cell?

a. It packages and distributes proteins.

b. It is the power source of the cell.

c. It makes sugar and oxygen.

d. It makes proteins.

10. What is the job of the lysosomes?

a. They store water.

b. They digest food particles

c. They make new cells.

d. They package proteins.

MATCHING

Read the description. Then, draw a line from the dot next to each description to the matching word.

11. a cell with a nucleus ●	**a.** DNA
12. a cell without a nucleus ●	**b.** eukaryote
13. genetic material in cells ●	**c.** nucleus
14. where DNA is stored ●	**d.** prokaryote

15. stiff surfaces that support cells ●	**a.** cell walls
16. organelle that makes proteins ●	**b.** endoplastmic reticulum
17. a cell's delivery system ●	**c.** ribosome

FILL-IN-THE-BLANK

Read the words in the box. Read the sentences. Fill in each blank with the word or phrase that best completes the sentence.

cell	multicellular	organ
structure	system	tissue

18. The lowest level of organization is the ______________________.

19. Cells that are like each other and do the same job form a(n) ______________________.

20. A structure made of two or more tissues working together is called a(n) ______________________.

21. A group of organs that work together form an organ ______________________.

22. Larger size, longer life, and more-specialized cells are characteristics of ______________________ organisms.

23. How a part of an organism works is related to how it is built, or its ______________________.

Name ______________________ Class ______________ Date ______________

Skills Worksheet

Directed Reading B

Section: Exchange with the Environment

Read the words in the box. Read the sentences. Fill in each blank with the word or phrase that best completes the sentence.

energy and raw materials	wastes
cell membrane	healthy

1. An organism must be able to take in

   ______________________________.

2. Materials move in and out of a cell through its

   ______________________________.

3. Taking in energy and getting rid of wastes keep an organism

   ______________________________.

4. An organism has to get rid of ______________________________.

WHAT IS DIFFUSION?

Circle the letter of the best answer for each question.

5. What is everything, including gelatin and dye, made up of?

   a. energy
   b. water
   c. heat
   d. tiny moving particles

6. Where will particles move when they are crowded?

   a. where it is warmer
   b. where it is cooler
   c. where it is less crowded
   d. where it is cleaner

7. What do we call particles moving from crowded areas to less crowded areas?

   a. diffusion
   b. flowing
   c. traveling
   d. exchanging

Circle the letter of the best answer for each question.

8. What don't cells need for diffusion?

a. food
b. water
c. energy
d. heat

Diffusion of Water

Read the description. Then, draw a line from the dot next to each description to the matching answer.

9. The fluids in an organism's cells are made mostly of this. ●

10. What particles that make up water are called. ●

11. What the diffusion of water is called. ●

12. Water moves through this during diffusion. ●

a. osmosis
b. cell membrane
c. water
d. molecules

The Cell and Osmosis

Circle the letter of the best answer for each question.

13. What is made up of water, salts, sugars, and other particles?

a. iced tea
b. cell membranes
c. molecules
d. plasma

14. What helps keep plasma in balance?

a. cold
b. heat
c. osmosis
d. energy

15. What does osmosis bring into the cells that helps wilted plant cells?

a. energy
b. water
c. sunlight
d. heat

MOVING SMALL PARTICLES

Circle the letter of the best answer for each question.

16. How do small particles cross a cell membrane?

a. through roadways

b. through channels

c. through holes

d. through pores

17. How do particles move from low concentration to high concentration?

a. active transport

b. passive transport

c. osmosis

d. diffusion

18. How do particles move from high to low concentration?

a. active transport

b. passive transport

c. osmosis

d. diffusion

19. What is a sac formed from pieces of cell membrane called?

a. endocytosis

b. vesicle

c. cell

d. particle

MOVING LARGE PARTICLES

Use the figure below to answer questions 20 and 21. Circle the letter of the best answer for each question.

Figure A

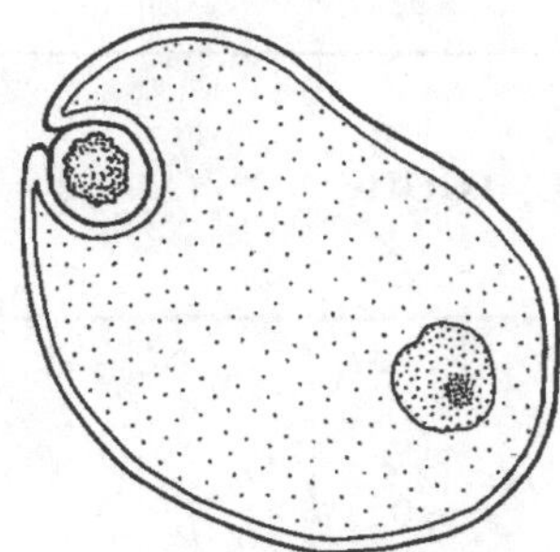

Figure B

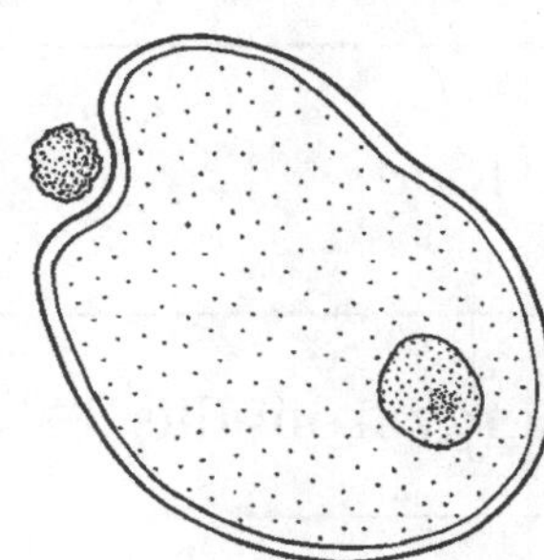

Figure C

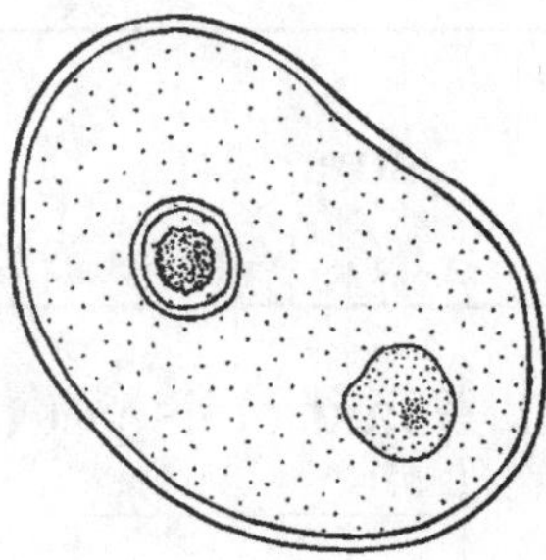

20. Look at the figure. A cell encloses a large particle in B, A, C order. What is the name of the process?

a. exocytosis

b. endocytosis

c. osmosis

d. diffusion

21. Look at the figure. A cell encloses a large particle in C, A, B order. What is the name of the process?

a. exocytosis

b. endocytosis

c. osmosis

d. diffusion

Name ______________________ Class ______________ Date ______________

Skills Worksheet

Directed Reading B

Section: Cell Energy

Read the words in the box. Read the sentences. Fill in each blank with the word or phrase that best completes the sentence.

sun	food	reproduce

1. Plant cells get their energy from the

______________________________.

2. Many animals get the energy they need from

______________________________.

3. All cells need energy to live, grow, and

______________________________.

FROM SUN TO CELL

the sun	food
energy	photosynthesis

4. Almost all of the energy used by living things comes from

______________________________.

5. Plants change energy from the sun into

______________________________.

6. The process that plants use to make food is called

______________________________.

7. Plants use the food they make for ______________________________ to live, grow, and reproduce.

Photosynthesis

Circle the letter of the best answer for each question.

8. In photosynthesis, what two things do plants use with sunlight to make food?

a. water and oxygen
b. water and sugar
c. water and carbon dioxide
d. water and salt

9. What food do plants make for themselves?

a. salt
b. glucose
c. chlorophyll
d. heat

GETTING ENERGY FROM FOOD

Read the words in the box. Read the sentences. Fill in each blank with the word or phrase that best completes the sentence.

cellular respiration	fermentation

10. Breaking down food for energy using oxygen is called

______________________________.

11. Breaking down food for energy without using oxygen is called

______________________________.

Cellular Respiration

Circle the letter of the best answer for each question.

12. How do most complex organisms get their energy?

a. through breathing
b. through eating
c. through sleeping
d. through cellular respiration

13. In cellular respiration, what do cells use to produce energy from food?

a. water
b. sunlight
c. oxygen
d. carbon dioxide

Circle the letter of the best answer for each question.

14. Which are broken down and released in cellular respiration?

a. water, carbon dioxide, and energy

b. water, energy, and oxygen

c. water, food, and carbon dioxide

d. water, oxygen, and food

Use the figure below to answer questions 15, 16, and 17. Circle the letter of the best answer for each question.

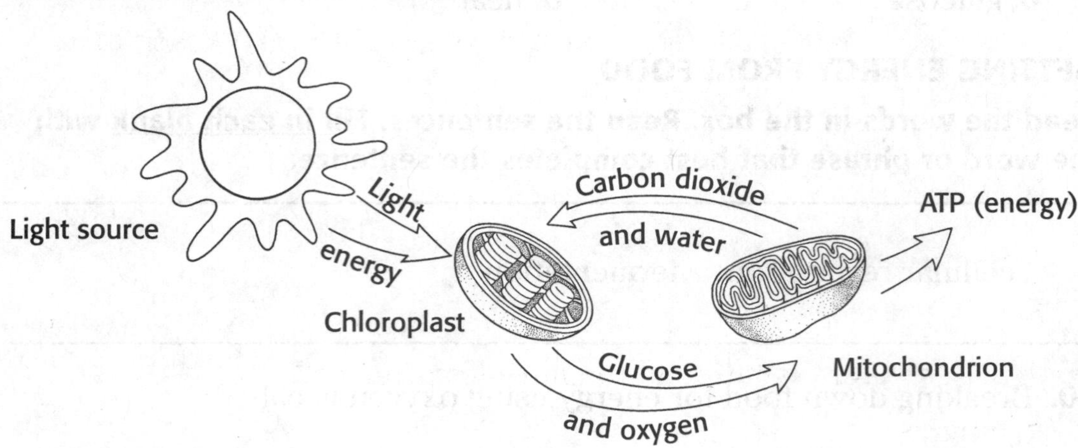

15. Look at the figure. What two processes does it show?

a. photosynthesis and breathing

b. breathing and growing

c. growing and cellular respiration

d. photosynthesis and cellular respiration

16. Look at the figure. Where does cellular respiration take place in the figure?

a. mitochondrion

b. cell membrane

c. fluids

d. chloroplast

17. Look at the figure. Besides energy, what else is released during cellular respiration?

a. carbon dioxide and oxygen

b. carbon dioxide and glucose

c. carbon dioxide and food

d. carbon dioxide and water

Connection Between Photosynthesis and Respiration

Read the description. Then, draw a line from the dot next to each description to the matching process.

18. Cells take in CO_2 carbon dioxide, and release oxygen ●

19. Cells use oxygen to break down food and release CO_2 ●

a. cellular respiration

b. photosynthesis

Fermentation

Circle the letter of the best answer for each question.

20. What do muscle cells use when they can't get oxygen for cellular respiration?

a. fermentation

b. photosynthesis

c. breathing

d. exercise

21. What does fermentation in the muscles produce?

a. fatigue

b. oxygen

c. cellular respiration

d. lactic acid

22. What does yeast form during fermentation?

a. lactic acid

b. carbon dioxide

c. glucose

d. bacteria

Name ______________________ Class ______________ Date ______________

Skills Worksheet

Directed Reading B

Section: The Cell Cycle

Circle the letter of the best answer for each question.

1. When your body makes new cells, what is being replaced?

a. water

b. energy

c. cells that have died

d. heat

2. What does making new cells allow you to do?

a. grow

b. sleep

c. eat

d. make food

THE LIFE OF A CELL

3. When does the cell cycle begin?

a. when the cell is formed

b. when the cell uses energy

c. when the cell divides

d. when the cell uses oxygen

4. When does the cell cycle end?

a. when the cell is formed

b. when the cell uses energy

c. when the cell divides

d. when the cell uses oxygen

5. What is the hereditary material inside a cell called?

a. nuclei

b. water

c. DNA

d. ATP

6. In what structures can cells' DNA be found?

a. bacteria

b. water

c. fluids

d. chromosomes

Making More Prokaryotic Cells

Read the words in the box. Read the sentences. Fill in each blank with the word or phrase that best completes the sentence.

more complex	less complex
binary fission	DNA

7. Prokaryotic cells, without nuclei, are

______________________ than eukaryotic cells.

8. Eukaryotic cells, with nuclei, are ______________________

than prokaryotic cells.

9. Prokaryotic cells such as bacteria divide by

______________________.

10. When binary fission is complete, each new cell has identical

______________________.

Eukaryotic Cells and Their DNA

Circle the letter of the best answer for each question.

11. How many chromosomes do humans have?

a. 8

b. 48

c. 32

d. 46

12. What are pairs of similar chromosomes called?

a. prokaryotic pairs

b. homologous chromosomes

c. DNA

d. eukaryotic pairs

Making More Eukaryotic Cells

<u>Circle the letter</u> of the best answer for each question.

13. How many stages does a eukaryotic cell cycle have?

a. two

b. three

c. four

d. five

14. When chromosomes are copied, what are the two copies called?

a. DNA

b. centromeres

c. chromatids

d. mitosis

15. When the chromosomes separate, what is the process called?

a. mitosis

b. copying

c. parting

d. duplicating

16. What does a cell do in the third stage of the cell cycle?

a. dies

b. divides into two identical cells

c. makes food

d. takes in oxygen

MITOSIS AND THE CELL CYCLE

Use the figure below to answer questions 17 through 20. Circle the letter of the best answer for each question.

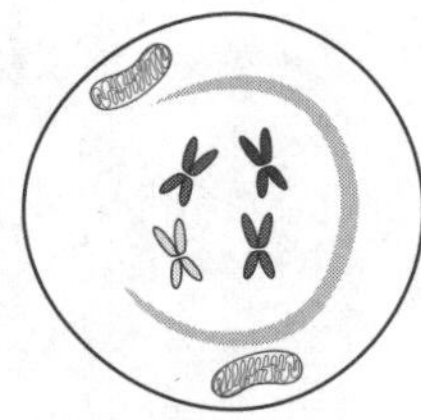
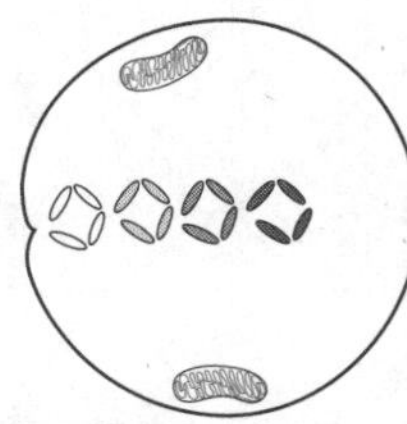
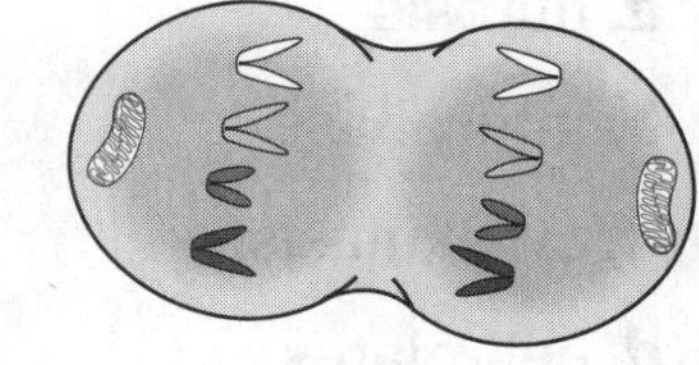

Mitosis Phase 1 Mitosis Phase 2 Mitosis Phase 3 Mitosis Phase 4

17. Look at the figure. When does mitosis begin and the chromosomes condense into rodlike structures?

a. Mitosis Phase 1 **c.** Mitosis Phase 3

b. Mitosis Phase 2 **d.** Mitosis Phase 4

18. Look at the figure. When do the chromatids separate and move to opposite sides of the cell?

a. Mitosis Phase 1 **c.** Mitosis Phase 3

b. Mitosis Phase 2 **d.** Mitosis Phase 4

19. Look at the figure. When does a nuclear membrane form around each set of chromosomes, completing mitosis?

a. Mitosis Phase 1 **c.** Mitosis Phase 3

b. Mitosis Phase 2 **d.** Mitosis Phase 4

20. Look at the figure. When do the chromosomes line up, and the homologous chromosomes pair up?

a. Mitosis Phase 1 **c.** Mitosis Phase 3

b. Mitosis Phase 2 **d.** Mitosis Phase 4

Cytokinesis

Circle the letter of the best answer for each question.

21. What is it called when the cytoplasm of a cell divides?

a. mitosis

b. interphase

c. cytokinesis

d. cell plates

22. What does the cell membrane do during cytokinesis in an animal cell?

a. pinches in two

b. forms a cell plate

c. makes copies of its DNA

d. shrivels up

23. What forms between the two new cells during plant cell cytokinesis?

a. cell plate

b. mitochondrion

c. chromatid

d. water

Name ______________________ Class ______________ Date ____________

Assessment

Chapter Test C

The Cell In Action

MULTIPLE CHOICE

Circle the letter of the best answer for each question.

1. What do all organisms need in order to live?

a. sunlight

b. exercise

c. energy and raw materials

d. shelter

2. What do all organisms need to get rid of in order to live?

a. wastes

b. heat

c. energy

d. fat

3. What do materials go in and out of an organism's cells through?

a. mouths

b. pores

c. mitochondria

d. cell membranes

4. What is the process that moves particles from areas of higher to areas of lower concentration called?

a. transportation

b. diffusion

c. active transport

d. travel

5. What is the process that moves particles from areas of lower to areas of higher concentration?

a. transportation

b. diffusion

c. active transport

d. osmosis

6. What helps wilted plants become firm during osmosis?

a. sunlight

b. water

c. energy

d. heat

MATCHING

Read the description. Then, draw a line from the dot next to each description to the matching answer.

7. Fluids in an organism's cells are made mostly of this. ●

8. This forms between two new cells during plant cell cytokinesis. ●

9. During this, water molecules move from higher to lower concentration. ●

10. Water moves through this in osmosis. ●

a. cell membrane

b. osmosis

c. water

d. cell plates

---

11. how plants make food with sunlight, CO_2, and water ●

12. how many animals get energy ●

13. the breakdown of food using oxygen ●

14. the breakdown of food without oxygen ●

a. fermentation

b. cellular respiration

c. food

d. photosynthesis

FILL-IN-THE-BLANK

Read the words in the box. Read the sentences. Fill in each blank with the word or phrase that best completes the sentence.

mitosis	chromosomes
homologous chromosomes	

15. Pairs of chromosomes are called ______________________.

16. Cells divide into two new cells by the process of ______________________.

17. Right before mitosis occurs, the ______________________ make copies of themselves.

exocytosis	fermentation
endocytosis	cellular respiration

18. In the process of ______________________, cells bring in large particles.

19. In the process of ______________________, cells remove large particles.

20. When oxygen breaks down food to release energy, it is called ______________________.

21. Breaking down food for energy without using oxygen is ______________________.

MULTIPLE CHOICE

Use the figure below to answer questions 22 and 23. Circle the letter of the best answer for each question.

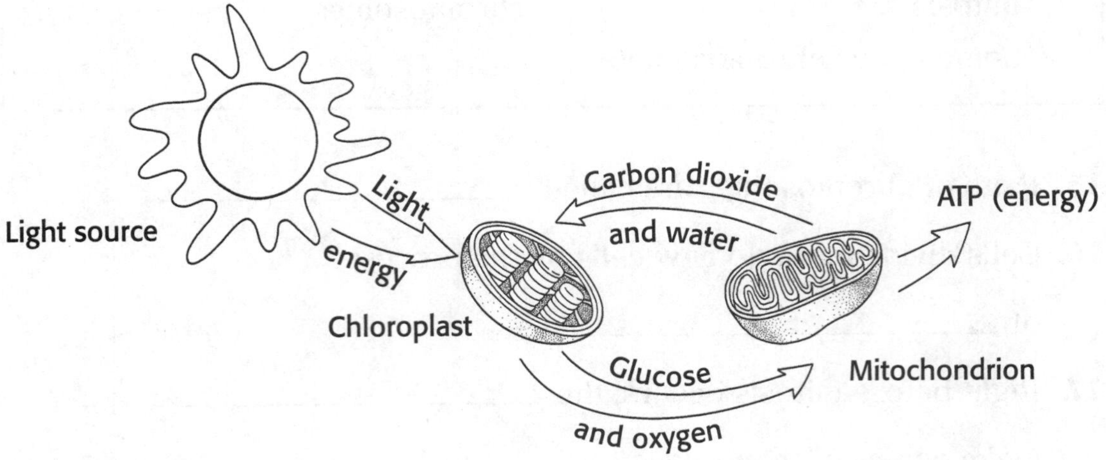

22. Look at the figure. What two processes does it show?

a. photosynthesis and breathing

b. breathing and growing

c. growing and cellular respiration

d. photosynthesis and cellular respiration

23. Look at the figure. What are released during cellular respiration?

a. carbon dioxide, oxygen, and energy

b. carbon dioxide, glucose, and energy

c. carbon dioxide, sweat, and energy

d. carbon dioxide, water, and energy

Name ______________________ Class ______________ Date ____________

Skills Worksheet

Directed Reading B

Section: Mendel and His Peas

Circle the letter of the best answer for each question.

1. What is heredity?

a. traits passing from offspring to parents

b. traits passing from parents to offspring

c. offspring with no genotypes

d. traits disappearing in offspring

WHO WAS GREGOR MENDEL?

2. In what country was Gregor Mendel born?

a. United States

b. Austria

c. Germany

d. Italy

3. Where did Gregor Mendel first learn about flowers and fruit trees?

a. in a lab

b. at a college

c. at a monastery

d. on a farm

4. Where did Gregor Mendel do his research?

a. in a lab

b. at a college

c. at a monastery

d. on a farm

UNRAVELING THE MYSTERY

Read the description. Then, draw a line from the dot next to each description to the matching word.

5. when a plant can fertilize itself ●	**a.** self-pollinating
6. when all offspring have the same traits as the parent ●	**b.** cross-pollinating
7. when one plant fertilizes another plant ●	**c.** true-breeding

8. different forms of characteristics ●	**a.** characteristics
9. used for Mendel's experiments ●	**b.** traits
10. different forms in a population ●	**c.** pea plants

MENDEL'S FIRST EXPERIMENTS

Read the words in the box. Read the sentences. Fill in each blank with the word or phrase that best completes the sentence.

recessive	dominant

11. A trait always seen in the first generation is the

______________________ trait.

12. A trait that reappears in the second generation is the

______________________ trait.

MENDEL'S SECOND EXPERIMENTS

Circle the letter of the best answer for each question.

13. What happened in the second generation, when Mendel allowed the first-generation plants to self-pollinate?

a. The dominant trait disappeared.

b. The recessive trait disappeared.

c. The dominant trait showed up.

d. The recessive trait showed up.

Ratios in Mendel's experiments

14. What is a ratio?

a. the second generation of a plant

b. the relationship between two different things

c. the cross-pollination of a plant

d. the passing of traits from parents to offspring

Gregor Mendel–Gone but Not Forgotten

15. When did Mendel get the recognition he deserved?

a. more than 30 years after his death

b. the day after he died

c. immediately after his experiments

d. 100 years after his death

Name ______________________ Class ______________ Date ______________

Skills Worksheet

Directed Reading B

Section: Traits and Inheritance

A GREAT IDEA

Circle the letter of the best answer for each question.

1. What is the ratio that Mendel found for dominant to recessive traits?

a. 1 to 1
b. 2 to 1
c. 3 to 1
d. 4 to 1

2. What do scientists call instructions for an inherited trait?

a. alleles
b. phenotype
c. albinism
d. genes

3. What are the two forms of a gene called?

a. alleles
b. phenotype
c. albinism
d. genes

Phenotype

4. What is a phenotype?

a. an inherited problem
b. a group of 10 alleles
c. a recessive gene
d. the way an organism looks

5. What prevents hair, skin, and eyes from having any color?

a. alleles
b. albinism
c. ratio
d. probability

Genotype

6. What are both inherited alleles together called?

a. an organism
b. a genotype
c. homozygous
d. heterozygous

Circle the letter of the best answer for each question.

7. What kind of plant has two dominant genes OR two recessive genes?
   a. an organism
   b. a genotype
   c. homozygous
   d. heterozygous

8. What kind of plant has one dominant gene AND one recessive gene?
   a. an organism
   b. a genotype
   c. homozygous
   d. heterozygous

Punnett Squares

Use the table below to answer questions 9 through 12. For each question, circle the letter of the best answer for each question.

	p	*p*
P	*Pp*	*Pp*
P	*Pp*	*Pp*

9. Look at the table above. What is this table called?
   a. P-grid
   b. dominance chart
   c. heredity map
   d. Punnett square

10. What is a Punnett square used for?
    a. to show recessive traits
    b. to show possible offspring
    c. to show dominant traits
    d. to show homozygous alleles

11. Look at the table above. If purple flower color (*P*) is dominant, what color will most of the offspring be?
    a. purple
    b. white
    c. same number of purple and white
    d. lavender (white and purple mix)

12. Look at the table above. What is the probability that the offspring will be *Pp*?
    a. 25%
    b. 50%
    c. 75%
    d. 100%

More Evidence for Inheritance

Circle the letter of the best answer for each question.

13. Which two combinations of genotypes are exactly the same?

a. *PP* and *Pp*

b. *Pp* and *pP*

c. *pp* and *Pp*

d. *pP* and *pp*

WHAT ARE THE CHANCES?

Probability

14. What is the chance of a parent with one green allele and one blue allele giving a blue allele to an offspring?

a. 100% chance

b. 25% chance

c. 50% chance

d. 75% chance

Read the description. Then, draw a line from the dot next to each description to the matching word.

15. the chance that something will happen ●

16. how probability is usually written ●

17. how to find probability ●

18. reason traits in pea plants are easy to predict ●

a. multiply

b. only two choices

c. fraction or percent

d. probability

MORE ABOUT TRAITS

Incomplete Dominance

Circle the letter of the best answer for each question.

19. What is it called when each allele has its own degree of influence?

a. incomplete dominance

b. complete dominance

c. cross-breeding

d. probability

One Gene, Many Traits

20. A white tiger's blue eyes are an example of what?

a. first-generation characteristic

b. dominant trait

c. many genes influencing one trait

d. one gene influencing more than one trait

Many Genes, One Trait

21. How many genes determine human eye color?

a. none

b. at least two

c. 1,000

d. one

The Importance of Environment

22. What can influence traits besides genes?

a. height

b. albinism

c. environment

d. phenotype

Name ______________________ Class ______________ Date ____________

Skills Worksheet

Directed Reading B

Section: Meiosis

Circle the letter of the best answer for each question.

1. What are the two kinds of reproduction?

a. chromosomes and offspring

b. heredity and genes

c. asexual and sexual

d. mothers and fathers

ASEXUAL REPRODUCTION

2. What is the name for the way cells divide in asexual reproduction?

a. twins

b. mitosis

c. meiosis

d. homologous

3. How many parent cells are needed in asexual reproduction?

a. one

b. two

c. 100

d. none

SEXUAL REPRODUCTION

4. How are offspring produced that are NOT like either parent?

a. by asexual reproduction

b. by something going wrong

c. by sexual reproduction

d. by mitosis

5. What do you call chromosomes that carry the same sets of genes?

a. twin chromosomes

b. homologous chromosomes

c. ordinary chromosomes

d. asexual chromosomes

6. How many chromosomes do human sex cells have?

a. 100

b. 23

c. one

d. none

Meiosis

Circle the letter of the best answer for each question.

7. What copying process makes cells with half the usual number of chromosomes?

a. sex cells
b. meiosis
c. a nucleus
d. mitosis

8. What is made during meiosis?

a. common human cells
b. sex cells
c. genes
d. chromosomes

Genes and Chromosomes

9. Where did Walter Sutton suggest that genes are found?

a. on offspring
b. in sex cells
c. in typical cells
d. on chromosomes

THE STEPS OF MEIOSIS

Read the description. Then, draw a line from the dot next to each description to the matching word.

10. exact copy of a chromosome ●
11. forms around each new cell ●
12. when the nucleus divides once ●
13. divides twice during meiosis ●

a. nucleus
b. mitosis
c. chromatoid
d. cell membranes

---

14. the first step in meiosis ●
15. how chromosomes get ready for cell to split ●
16. the last step in meiosis ●
17. the second step in meiosis ●

a. four cells formed from one cell
b. chromosomes line up at the center of cell
c. chromosomes make copy of selves
d. chromosomes pair up

MEIOSIS AND MENDEL

Read the words in the box. Read the sentences. Fill in each blank with the word or phrase that best completes the sentence.

Y chromosome	X chromosomes
hemophilia	meiosis

18. The steps in ______________________ explain Mendel's results.

Sex Chromosomes

19. Females have two ______________________ and males have one X and one Y.

20. When males give a(n) ______________________ the offspring will be male.

Sex-Linked Disorders

21. A sex-linked blood-clotting disorder found mostly in males is ______________________.

Genetic Counseling

Read the words in the box. Read the sentences. Fill in each blank with the word or phrase that best completes the sentence.

carriers	selective breeding
recessive	pedigree

22. To trace a family trait through many years, you can use a diagram called a ______________________________.

23. A genetic counselor can often predict ______________________________ of hereditary diseases.

24. People with cystic fibrosis have two ______________________________ alleles.

Selective Breeding

25. Large eggs and large flowers are both created through ______________________________.

Name ______________________ Class ______________ Date ____________

Assessment

Chapter Test C

Heredity

MULTIPLE CHOICE

Circle the letter of the best answer for each question.

1. What is heredity?

a. traits passing from offspring to parents

b. traits passing from parents to offspring

c. plants that are cross-pollinated

d. the ratio of dominant to recessive traits

2. What is a plant that has two dominant genes or two recessive genes called ?

a. organism

b. genotype

c. homozygous

d. heterozygous

3. What is Mendel's ratio for dominant to recessive traits?

a. 1 to 1

b. 2 to 1

c. 3 to 1

d. 4 to 1

4. What is a phenotype?

a. the way an organism feels

b. a group of 5 alleles

c. a dominant gene

d. the way an organism looks

5. What is it called when cells are copied with half the number of chromosomes?

a. sex cells

b. meiosis

c. a nucleus

d. mitosis

MATCHING

Read the description. Then, draw a line from the dot next to each description to the matching word.

6. when each allele has its own degree of dominance	**a.** self-pollinating
7. when all offspring that have same traits as parent	**b.** incomplete dominance
8. made during meiosis	**c.** sex cells
9. a plant that fertilizes itself	**d.** true-breeding plants

10. exact copy of a chromosome	**a.** probability
11. the chance that something will happen	**b.** fraction or percent
12. how chromosomes get ready for the cell to split	**c.** line up at center of cell
13. how probability is usually written	**d.** chromatid

FILL-IN-THE-BLANK

Read the words in the box. Read the sentences. Fill in each blank with the word or phrase that best completes the sentence.

genes	pedigree	color blindness
X chromosomes		

14. Sometimes, two or more ______________________ work together to decide one trait.

15. Females have two ______________________ and males have one X and one Y.

16. To trace a family trait through many years, you can use a ______________________.

17. Men only have one set of X chromosome genes. Because of this, they are more likely to have ______________________.

MULTIPLE CHOICE

Use the table below to answer questions 18–20. For each question, circle the letter of the best answer for each question.

	P	*p*
P	*PP*	*Pp*
p	*Pp*	*pp*

______ **18.** Look at the table. What is this table called?

a. P-grid

b. dominance chart

c. heredity map

d. Punnett square

______ **19.** Look at the diagram. If purple *(P)* is dominant, and white *(p)* is recessive, what color will one out of every four of the offspring be?

a. purple

b. white

c. purple with white edges

d. lavender (white and purple mix)

______ **20.** Look at the table. What is the probability that the offspring will be *pp*?

a. 25%

b. 50%

c. 75%

d. 100%

Name ______________________ Class ______________ Date ____________

Skills Worksheet

Directed Reading B

Section: What Does DNA Look Like?

Circle the letter of the best answer for each question.

1. Which of the following passes on inherited characteristics?

a. parts

b. genes

c. cells

d. puzzles

2. What is the shorter way to say deoxyribonucleic acid?

a. DNA **c.** DEO

b. RAN **d.** DAR

3. What are genes a part of?

a. molecules

b. amino acids

c. chromosomes

d. protein

THE PIECES OF THE PUZZLE

4. What does DNA tell a cell to do?

a. build a new cell

b. become a chromosome

c. surprise scientists

d. become more complex

`5. When must material that makes up genes be copied?

a. when it grows bigger

b. when scientists need it

c. each time a cell divides

d. when proteins are in it

Nucleotides: The Subunits of DNA

Read the words in the box. Read the sentences. Fill in each blank with the word that best completes the sentence.

nucleotides	guanine
thymine	cytosine

6. The DNA subunits called ______________________ have a sugar, a phosphate, and a base.

7. The four kinds of bases are adenine, thymine, ______________________, and cytosine.

Chargaff's Rules

8. Chargaff found that the amount of adenine in DNA equals the amount of ______________________.

9. Chargaff found that the amount of guanine in DNA equals the amount of ______________________.

Franklin's Discovery

Circle the letter of the best answer for each question.

10. What did Rosalind Franklin show about DNA molecules?

a. their scientific history

b. their spiral shape

c. their cytosine

d. their rules

Watson and Crick's Model

Circle the letter of the best answer for each question.

11. What did Watson and Crick think DNA looked like?

a. a model

b. a long, twisted ladder

c. a mysterious substance

d. a copy of a protein

12. What did Watson and Crick build to help explain DNA?

a. an X ray

b. a material

c. a model

d. a cell

DNA'S DOUBLE STRUCTURE

Read the words in the box. Read the sentences. Fill in each blank with the word or phrase that best completes the sentence.

cytosine	double helix
bases	thymine

13. The twisted ladder shape of DNA is called

a ______________________________.

14. The rungs of the ladder are made of a pair

of ______________________________.

15. Guanine pairs with ______________________________.

16. Adenine pairs with ______________________________.

MAKING COPIES OF DNA

Circle the letter of the best answer for each question.

17. When cells can replicate, what do they do?

a. grow

b. make bases

c. make new cells

d. bond with anything

How Copies Are Made

18. How is a DNA molecule split as it is copied?

a. down the middle

b. by a strand

c. top to bottom

d. by the sugars

19. What are the bases on each part of the split DNA used for?

a. a sugar

b. a phosphate

c. a pattern

d. a protein

When Copies Are Made

20. When is DNA copied?

a. when a nucleus gets big

b. when there are no proteins

c. when it is read

d. every time a cell divides

21. What helps DNA copy itself?

a. proteins

b. phosphates

c. cells

d. strands

Name ______________________ Class ______________ Date ______________

Skills Worksheet

Directed Reading B

Section: How DNA Works

UNRAVELING DNA

Circle the letter of the best answer for each question.

1. What is DNA often bundled into?

a. proteins

b. chromosomes

c. bases

d. traits

2. What is a string of nucleotides called?

a. traits

b. loops

c. a cell

d. a gene

3. How many genes do humans have?

a. 100

b. 300

c. at least 30,000

d. 1,000

4. How many chromosomes does a cell have before dividing?

a. unlimited

b. 23

c. 46

d. 12

GENES AND PROTEINS

Circle the letter of the best answer for each question.

5. What do three bases form?

a. DNA

b. genes

c. chromatin

d. amino acids

6. What does each gene have instructions for making?

a. protein

b. cells

c. amino acids

d. DNA

Proteins and Traits

7. What do proteins act as?

a. organism

b. bases

c. codes

d. chemical triggers and messengers

Help from RNA

8. What other type of molecule helps make proteins?

a. RAD

b. RNA

c. DNR

d. DTR

The Making of a Protein

Read the words in the box. Read the sentences. Fill in each blank with the word or phrase that best completes the sentence.

ribosome	transfer RNA
messenger RNA	

9. A mirrorlike copy of a DNA segment is called ______________________.

10. The RNA copy goes through a protein assembly line or ______________________.

11. The message is translated by ______________________ and a protein is made.

CHANGES IN GENES

Mutations

Circle the letter of the best answer for the question.

12. Changes in the bases of DNA are called what?
   - **a.** extras
   - **b.** roller coasters
   - **c.** accidents
   - **d.** mutations

Read the words in the box. Read the sentences. Fill in each blank with the word or phrase that best completes the sentence.

deletion	substitution
insertion	

13. When a base is left out, the change is called a(n) ______________________________.

14. When an extra base is added, the change is called a(n) ______________________________.

15. When the wrong base is used, the change is called a(n) ______________________________.

Do Mutations Matter?

Circle the letter of the best answer for each question.

16. Which of these does not result from mutation?

a. an improvement

b. a harmful change

c. cell repair

d. no change

How Do Mutations Happen?

17. What is one way mutations happen?

a. because of ribosomes

b. because DNA wears out

c. because of random errors

d. because of sugars

Circle the letter of the best answer for each question.

18. What are agents that might damage DNA called?

a. ribosome

b. mutagen

c. generation

d. regulation

AN EXAMPLE OF SUBSTITUTION

19. What can a mutation produce?

a. a bad sunburn

b. transfer RNA

c. the wrong protein

d. cigarette smoke

20. What is one example of a substitution mutation?

a. blue eyes

b. sickle cell anemia

c. height

d. red hair

USES OF GENETIC KNOWLEDGE

Genetic Engineering

21. What is it called when scientists change an organism's genes?

a. DNA fingerprinting

b. genetic engineering

c. genetics

d. transfer RNA

Circle the letter of the best answer for each question.

22. What happened when scientists added a firefly gene to a plant?

a. The firefly glowed.

b. The plant died.

c. The plant glowed.

d. The plant vanished.

Genetic Identification

23. How are the unique patterns in DNA identified?

a. DNA fingerprinting

b. genetic engineering

c. genetics

d. transfer RNA

24. What is an organism that has an exact copy of another's DNA called?

a. a twin

b. a brother or sister

c. a clone

d. a child or offspring

Name ______________________ Class ______________ Date ______________

Assessment

Chapter Test C

Genes and DNA

MULTIPLE CHOICE

Circle the letter of the best answer for each question.

1. Which of these is a subunit of DNA?

a. RNA

b. trait

c. ribosome

d. nucleotide

2. Along with a sugar and a phosphate, what is the third part of a nucleotide?

a. a base

b. a protein

c. a chromosome

d. a ribosome

3. Who said that adenine equals thymine in DNA?

a. Rosalind Franklin

b. James Watson

c. Erwin Chargaff

d. Francis Crick

4. Who first found out that DNA has a spiral shape?

a. Rosalind Franklin

b. James Watson

c. Erwin Chargaff

d. Francis Crick

Circle the letter of the best answer for each question.

5. What does DNA look like?

a. a ball

b. a straight line

c. links in a chain

d. a twisted ladder

6. What is a string of nucleotides called?

a. a ribosome

b. a gene

c. a transfer RNA

d. a chromosome

7. What does each gene have instructions for making?

a. a cell

b. a ribosome

c. a protein

d. RNA

8. Where does messenger RNA go?

a. to a protein

b. to a genetic engineer

c. to a ribosome

d. to a chromosome

MATCHING

Read the description. Then draw a line from the dot next to each description to the matching word.

9. a change in a gene	●	**a.** DNA
10. a copy of part of a DNA strand	●	**b.** mutation
11. a subunit of DNA	●	**c.** nucleotide
12. deoxyribonucleic acid	●	**d.** RNA

13. the "factory" that creates new proteins	●	**a.** messenger RNA
14. the RNA that translates the messenger RNA message	●	**b.** ribosome
15. the RNA that is a copy of part of a DNA strand	●	**c.** transfer RNA
16. changes in DNA that can cause problems	●	**d.** mutations

FILL-IN-THE-BLANK

Read the words in the box. Read the sentences. Fill in each blank with the word or phrase that best completes the sentence.

guanine	complementary
replicate	thymine

17. Pairs of bases match up because they are

______________________________ to each other.

18. The pairing of bases allows cells to ______________________________.

19. Adenine and ______________________________ bases fit together.

20. Cytosine and ______________________________ bases fit together.

Name ______________________ Class ______________ Date ____________

Skills Worksheet

Directed Reading B

Section: Change Over Time

DIFFERENCES AMONG ORGANISMS

Read the description. Then, draw a line from the dot next to each description to the matching word.

1. a characteristic that helps a plant or animal survive •

2. a group of plants or animals that can mate with one another •

3. members of the same species that live in the same place •

a. species

b. adaptation

c. population

Do Species Change Over Time?

Circle the letter of the best answer for each question.

4. How many different species are there?

a. dozens
b. hundreds
c. thousands
d. millions

5. Why are many species no longer on Earth?

a. They turned into fossils.
b. They died out.
c. They adapted.
d. They turned into populations.

6. What do scientists think happens as populations change over time?

a. Species stay the same.
b. New species form.
c. Fossils die out.
d. Evolution stops.

7. What is it called when plants or animals slowly change over time?

a. evolution
b. population
c. reproduction
d. organization

EVIDENCE OF CHANGES OVER TIME

Circle the letter of the best answer for each question.

8. Where is evidence of evolution found?

a. in the atmosphere of Earth

b. in the sands carried by desert winds

c. in the layers of the Earth

d. in the falling rain

Fossils

9. What are fossils?

a. the remains of plants and animals that once lived

b. adaptations

c. layers of Earth

d. old rocks

The Fossil Record

10. What helps to make fossils?

a. dirt

b. plaster

c. water

d. sediment

11. What is the fossil record?

a. the rocks that cover fossils

b. a book about fossils

c. a timeline of life

d. the minerals that form fossils

12. What does the fossil record tell us?

a. how old rocks are

b. when fossil species lived

c. how many rock layers the Earth has

d. what minerals make good fossils

Circle the letter of the best answer for each question.

13. What do we know about fossils found in newer layers of Earth?

a. They are the oldest fossils.

b. They are close relatives of organisms alive now.

c. They are imprints.

d. They are not really fossils yet.

EVIDENCE OF ANCESTRY

14. What do scientists think that all living species descended from?

a. trees

b. traits

c. ancestors

d. fossils

15. What do all living things get from ancestors?

a. traits

b. evolution

c. fossils

d. offspring

Drawing Connections

16. What model do scientists use to draw the fossil record?

a. a diagram with branches

b. a diagram with circles

c. a horizontal timeline

d. a bar graph

17. How does a new species show up on the model?

a. as a circle

b. as a fruit

c. as a branch

d. as a trunk

Read the description. Then, draw a line from the dot next to each description to the matching word.

18. something that tells the order in which species lived ●

19. a model showing all known plant and animal species ●

20. the rare remains of animals or plants ●

a. the fossil record

b. fossils

c. tree of life

EXAMINING ORGANISMS

Read the words in the box. Read the sentences. <u>Fill in each blank</u> with the word or phrase that best completes the sentence.

water	fossil record	land
ancestors	limbs	mammals

21. Studying a plant or animal very closely can give clues about its

______________________.

22. Whales are ______________________, not fish.

23. Whales had an ancient ancestor that lived on

______________________.

24. Whales do not have hind ______________________ anymore, but they still have some of the bones.

25. Whales had another ancestor that lived both on land and in

______________________.

26. A sequence of fossils in the ______________________ links ancient mammals to modern whales.

COMPARING ORGANISMS

<u>Circle the letter</u> of the best answer for the question.

27. What can comparing different groups of animals show?

a. their identical adaptations

b. their common ancestry

c. their identical evolution

d. their ability to mate with each other

Circle the letter of the best answer for each question.

28. What do all plants and animals get from their ancestors?

a. learned behaviors

b. hind limbs

c. front limbs

d. traits and DNA

Comparing Skeletal Structure

29. How is your hand like a bat's wing?

a. Your hands have similar bones.

b. Your hand does similar things.

c. Your hand has similar muscles.

d. Your hand looks the same.

30. Why does your hand have almost the same bones as a dolphin's flipper?

a. Dolphins evolved from people.

b. Dolphins and people have a common ancestor.

c. People evolved from dolphins.

d. Flippers are the same as hands.

Comparing DNA

31. What is a sign that tigers and cats might have a common ancestor?

a. They have similar genetic information.

b. They have similar looks.

c. They have similar environments.

d. They have similar size.

Name ______________________ Class ______________ Date ______________

Skills Worksheet

Directed Reading B

Section: How Does Evolution Happen?

Circle the letter of the best answer for each question.

1. What did scientists begin to realize in the 1800s?

a. Earth was much larger than people had thought.

b. Earth was much warmer than people had thought.

c. Earth was much younger than people had thought.

d. Earth was much older than people had thought.

CHARLES DARWIN

2. What did Darwin do to learn about plants and animals?

a. He took a trip around the world.

b. He read books.

c. He made up theories.

d. He bought animals.

Darwin's Excellent Adventure

3. What did Darwin do during his travels?

a. He wrote a book about his theory.

b. He collected thousands of plant and animal samples.

c. He took photos of plants and animals.

d. He visited all the continents.

Darwin's Finches

4. The plants and animals in the Galápagos Islands were like those in which of the following?

a. England

b. Ecuador

c. Australia

d. South Africa

Circle the letter of the best answer for each question.

5. What did Darwin find out about the finches?

a. They were hungry.

b. They were on the wrong islands.

c. Similar finches had different beaks.

d. Some finches could not fly.

6. What did the different kinds of beaks allow the finches to do?

a. find mates

b. get food

c. fly

d. hide

DARWIN'S THINKING

7. What did Darwin do after his trip?

a. He studied the evidence for many years.

b. He announced his discovery right away.

c. He took another trip around the world.

d. He gave up.

8. What did Darwin decide about the finches?

a. They had the wrong beaks for the islands.

b. They would not survive on the islands.

c. They had adapted to different ways of life.

d. They had not adapted to different ways of life.

Ideas About Breeding

9. Why might selective breeding be used for horses?

a. to show natural selection

b. to slow evolution

c. to make horses faster or bigger

d. to make horses worse animals

Circle the letter of the best answer for each question.

10. Why might selective breeding be used for fruit trees?

a. to show natural selection

b. to slow evolution

c. to make fruit taste bad

d. to make bigger fruit

11. Which of these is NOT a result of selective breeding?

a. wings on bats

b. faster horses

c. different breeds of dogs

d. larger fruit

Read the description. Then, draw a line from the dot next to each description to the matching word.

12. characteristics that can be passed from parents to offspring through genes ●	**a.** selective breeding
13. process of producing plants and animals with better traits ●	**b.** traits

Ideas About Population

Read the words in the box. Read the sentences. Fill in each blank with the word or phrase that best completes the sentence.

limited	inherit	populations

14. Thomas Malthus warned that ______________________ can grow faster than the food supply.

15. Darwin realized that species are ______________________ by starvation, disease, and other things.

16. Darwin thought that survivors in a species ______________________ traits that help them survive.

Ideas About Earth's History

Read the words in the box. Read the sentences. Fill in each blank with the word or phrase that best completes the sentence.

older	old
long	evolve

17. Darwin began to think that species could

______________________________ over time.

18. Evolution involves slow change. Some people thought that Earth was not ______________________________ enough for slow changes.

19. Darwin read a book that showed that Earth had formed over a

______________________________ period of time.

20. After reading the book, Darwin knew that Earth was

______________________________ than anyone had thought.

DARWIN'S THEORY OF NATURAL SELECTION

Circle the letter of the best answer for each question.

21. What did Darwin call the process by which evolution takes place?

a. genetic change

b. inheritance

c. limitation

d. natural selection

22. How many parts does the process of natural selection have?

a. 1

b. 2

c. 4

d. 6

Name ______________________ Class ______________ Date ____________

Read the description. Then, draw a line from the dot next to each description to the matching word.

23. when animals have too many offspring	●	**a.** successful reproduction
24. when no offspring are exactly the same	●	**b.** inherited variation
25. when many offspring die before they can reproduce	●	**c.** struggle to survive
26. when the best adapted offspring survive and reproduce	●	**d.** overproduction

Genetics and Evolution

27. may change when organisms produce produce offspring	●	**a.** selection
28. process that occurs only when organisms survive to reproduce	●	**b.** genes
29. add to understanding of evolution and natural selection	●	**c.** fossil discoveries

Name ______________________ Class ____________ Date ____________

Skills Worksheet

Directed Reading B

Section: Natural Selection in Action

CHANGES IN POPULATIONS

Circle the letter of the best answer for each question.

1. What theory explains how a population changes when the place it lives in changes?

a. adaptation

b. resistance

c. natural selection

d. speciation

2. Besides surviving, what will the best adapted members of a population do?

a. die out

b. reproduce

c. grow

d. hunt

Adaptation to Hunting

3. Why do people hunt elephants for their tusks?

a. so they can catch female elephants

b. because tusks are not valuable

c. because tusks are valuable to people

d. so they can breed more elephants

4. Why is the number of elephants born without tusks in Uganda increasing?

a. because fewer elephants with tusks live to reproduce

b. because more elephants with tusks live to reproduce

c. because fewer tuskless elephants live to reproduce

d. because elephants without tusks can't reproduce

Insecticide Resistance

<u>Circle the letter</u> of the best answer for each question.

5. What is the average time between one generation and the next called?

a. offspring time

b. reproduction time

c. replacement time

d. generation time

6. Why do some insects quickly develop insecticide resistance?

a. They have long wing spans.

b. They have short generation times.

c. They have long generation times.

d. They have few offspring.

Read the words in the box. Read the sentences. <u>Fill in each blank</u> with the word or phrase that best completes the sentence.

insecticide	resistant
genes	offspring

7. A few insects may survive an insecticide. This is because they have

______________________ that make them resistant to it.

8. These survivors pass on insecticide-resistant genes to their

______________________.

9. In time, most of the insects will have the

______________________- resistant genes.

10. Then, the same insecticide will kill only a few insects because the

rest are ______________________ to it.

Competition for Mates

Circle the letter of the best answer for each question.

11. What can competition for mates in a species lead to?

a. strong resistance

b. interesting adaptations

c. sudden death

d. generation time

FORMING A NEW SPECIES

Read the words in the box. Read the sentences. Fill in each blank with the word or phrase that best completes the sentence.

speciation	separation	adaptations

12. The forming of a new species by evolution is called

______________________.

Separation

13. When a part of a population moves away from the other it is called

______________________.

Adaptation

14. If plants or animals face different environments, they will have

different ______________________.

Division

<u>Circle the letter</u> of the best answer for each question.

15. When separated groups of a population can no longer interbreed, what process has just happened?

a. adaptation

b. separation

c. reproduction

d. division

16. When do two groups stop being in the same species?

a. when they live in different places

b. when they change color or grow feathers

c. when they can't mate with each other

d. when they eat different foods

17. What is one reason that two kinds of frogs can no longer mate?

a. They now mate at different times of the year.

b. They have not adapted to each other.

c. They compete for food and mates.

d. They have too many offspring.

Name ______________________ Class ______________ Date ____________

Assessment

Chapter Test C

The Evolution of Living Things

MULTIPLE CHOICE

Circle the letter of the best answer for each question.

1. What are the buried remains of animals and plants called?

a. adaptations
b. fossils
c. genetics
d. offspring

2. What does speciation create?

a. offspring
b. ancestors
c. a new species
d. resistance

3. What can two different species have in common?

a. populations
b. ancestors
c. individuals
d. offspring

4. What did Charles Darwin help to explain?

a. the age of Earth
b. how species change over time
c. how fossils are formed
d. genetics

5. Which of the following did NOT help Darwin create his theory?

a. the age Earth
b. the birds of the Galápagos
c. knowledge of genetics
d. selective breeding of dogs and horses

6. What helps a plant or animal survive in its environment?

a. adaptations
b. separations
c. divisions
d. resistances

Circle the letter of the best answer for each question.

7. What is a trait?

a. a kind of fossil

b. a genetic change

c. a new species

d. a characteristic parents give to offspring

8. Which of the following is NOT a result of natural selection?

a. horses that are bred to be faster

b. insects that are able to resist insecticides

c. bacteria that survive antibiotics

d. elephants that are born without tusks

9. Sometimes part of a population moves away from the rest. What is this called?

a. division

b. adaptation

c. separation

d. genetic change

10. What is it called when separated groups of a population cannot mate with each other?

a. division

b. interbreeding

c. resistance

d. selective breeding

11. Which of the following do scientists think was an ancestor of whales?

a. a large tree

b. an ancient fish

c. a shark

d. an ancient land mammal

MATCHING

Read the description. Then, draw a line from the dot next to each description to the matching word.

12. The best adapted offspring live and reproduce.

13. Organisms face competition, hunger, and predators.

14. Parents have too many offspring.

15. All offspring are different from each other.

a. inherited variation

b. struggle to survive

c. overpopulation

d. successful reproduction

FILL-IN-THE-BLANK

Read the words in the box. Read the sentences. Fill in each blank with the word or phrase that best completes the sentence.

species	population	selective breeding
evolution	fossil record	generation time

16. Mating animals so their offspring will inherit desired traits is called

______________________________.

17. Slow changes in animals and plants over time is known as

______________________________.

18. A group that can mate and have fertile offspring is a(n)

______________________________.

19. The time between one generation of offspring and the next is

______________________________.

20. Members of a species who live in the same place are a(n)

______________________________.

21. The history of life shown by fossils is the

______________________________.

Name ______________________________ Class ______________ Date ____________

Skills Worksheet

Directed Reading B

Section: Evidence of the Past

Circle the letter of the best answer for each question.

1. What are scientists who study life before humans existed called?

a. fossilologists

b. dinosaurologists

c. sedimentologists

d. paleontologists

FOSSILS

2. What are imprints of living things that are preserved in rock called?

a. sediment

b. fossils

c. dinosaurs

d. fungi

THE AGE OF FOSSILS

Read the words in the box. Read the sentences. Fill in each blank with the word or phrase that best completes the sentence.

relative	atoms	absolute

3. Estimating the age of fossils by where they are found is called

________________________________ dating.

4. Measuring the age of fossils in years is called

________________________________ dating.

5. To measure a fossil's age exactly, scientists study particles of matter

called ________________________________.

THE GEOLOGIC TIME SCALE

Circle the letter of the best answer for each question.

6. What does the geologic time scale show about Earth?

a. its unit

b. its grade

c. its history

d. its formation

7. How do scientists put fossils in order on the geologic time scale?

a. by date

b. at the bottom

c. at the top

d. by kind

Divisions in the Geologic Time Scale

8. What are the biggest blocks of time in the geologic time scale called?

a. fossils

b. eras

c. reptiles

d. organisms

Mass Extinctions

9. What kind of event made some divisions in the geologic time scale?

a. A species died out.

b. A volcano erupted.

c. A species reappeared.

d. A species moved.

10. What is it called when many species suddenly die out?

a. dinosaur extinction

b. fossil extinction

c. mass extinction

d. extreme extinction

THE CHANGING EARTH

Circle the letter of the best answer for each question.

11. Where do fossils show Antarctica was long ago?

a. in North America

b. in the Arctic Circle

c. near the equator

d. near Pangaea

Pangaea

12. Where did Wegener think the continents were long ago?

a. in Antarctica

b. in one landmass

c. under the ocean

d. where they are now

13. What is the large landmass all continents may have belonged to long ago called?

a. tectonic plate

b. continental plates

c. Pangaea

d. Africa

Do the Continents Move?

Read the words in the box. Read the sentences. Fill in each blank with the word or phrase that best completes the sentence.

plate tectonics	tectonic plate

14. Each huge piece of the Earth's crust is called a

______________________.

15. The idea of how Earth's crust moves around the Earth is called

______________________.

Adaptation to Slow Changes

Circle the letter of the best answer for each question.

16. What may happen to living things when Earth's conditions change very quickly?

a. Living things adapt.

b. Living things become extinct.

c. Living things become forests.

d. Living things grow.

17. What is an example of a rapid change of conditions on Earth?

a. dinosaurs evolving

b. continents moving

c. a meteorite hits the Earth

d. living things adapting

18. What is an example of a slow change of conditions on Earth?

a. mass extinction

b. continents moving

c. a meteorite hits the Earth

d. tropical forests growing

19. What may happen when Earth changes slowly?

a. some organisms survive

b. animals go to Antarctica

c. meteorites strike

d. mass extinctions

Name ______________________ Class ______________ Date ____________

Skills Worksheet

Directed Reading B

Section: Eras of the Geologic Time Scale

Circle the letter of the best answer for each question.

1. What are the four biggest eras in geologic history?

a. Precambrian, Paleozoic, Mesozoic, and Cenozoic

b. Precambrian, Prehistoric, Mesozoic, and Cenozoic

c. Prehistoric, Mesozoic, and Cenozoic, and Modern

d. Prehistoric, Paleozoic, Mesozoic, and Modern

PRECAMBRIAN TIME

2. What first appeared on Earth during Precambrian time?

a. dinosaurs

b. mammals

c. life

d. humans

How Did Life Begin?

3. What do scientists think the earliest living things grew from?

a. oxygen

b. a nucleus

c. simple chemicals

d. photosynthesis

4. How many cells did the first living things, prokaryotes, have?

a. none

b. one

c. hundreds

d. thousands

Photosynthesis and Oxygen

Read the description. Then draw a line from the dot next to each description to the matching word.

5. living things that first made food from sunlight ●

6. gas that cyanobacteria sent into oceans and air ●

7. a layer of gas around the earth that keeps out radiation ●

a. cyanobacteria

b. ozone

c. oxygen

Multicellular Organisms

Circle the letter of the best answer for each question.

8. A billion years after Earth formed, what kind of living things appeared?

a. smaller, less complex

b. gas

c. larger, more complex

d. fossil

9. What may eukaryotic cells have evolved into?

a. organisms made of many cells

b. organisms made of one cell

c. prokaryotes

d. fossils

THE PALEOZOIC ERA

10. What geologic era came after the Precambrian era?

a. Mesozoic

b. Paleozoic

c. Modern

d. Prehistoric

Circle the letter of the best answer for each question.

11. What do Paleozoic era rocks have a lot of?

a. sand

b. fossils

c. fish

d. dirt

12. What were the first animals to have a backbone?

a. sponges

b. humans

c. fish

d. mammals

13. What does the word *Paleozoic* mean?

a. new life

b. ancient life

c. animal life

d. no life

Life on Land

14. During the Paleozoic era plants and animals slowly moved where?

a. into the air

b. onto the land

c. into the oceans

d. into shelter

15. What were some of the first animals to live on land?

a. salamanders

b. reptiles

c. crawling insects

d. winged insects

Circle the letter of the best answer for each question.

16. What happened to almost all living things from the Paleozoic era?

a. They came to land.

b. They moved to the oceans.

c. They died out.

d. They were eaten.

THE MESOZOIC ERA

17. What era came after the Paleozoic Era?

a. the Prehistoric era

b. the Precambrian era

c. the Mesozoic era

d. the Modern era

18. What is the Mesozoic Era known as?

a. The Age of Fossils

b. The Age of Reptiles

c. The Age of Fishes

d. The Age of Plants

Life in the Mesozoic Era

19. What are the best-known reptiles of the Mesozoic era?

a. salamanders

b. birds

c. dinosaurs

d. plants

The Extinction of Dinosaurs

Circle the letter of the best answer for each question.

20. What is one theory about why of the dinosaurs died out?

a. A meteorite caused changes.

b. There was too much sunlight.

c. The dinosaurs got sick.

d. Earth's temperatures got higher.

THE CENOZOIC ERA

Read the description. Then, draw a line from the dot next to each description to the matching word.

21. the geologic era that followed the Mesozoic ●

22. what *Cenozoic* means in Greek ●

23. type of animals the Cenozoic era is famous for ●

a. mammals

b. recent life

c. Cenozoic

The Cenozoic Era Today

Circle the letter of the best answer for each question.

24. What happened during the Cenozoic Era?

a. Dinosaurs appeared.

b. Mammals disappeared.

c. Dinosaurs disappeared.

d. Modern humans appeared.

Name ______________________ Class ______________ Date ____________

Skills Worksheet

Directed Reading B

Section: Humans and Other Primates

PRIMATES

<u>Circle the letter</u> **of the best answer for each question.**

1. What group of mammals do apes, monkeys, lemurs, and humans belong to?

a. primates

b. cold-blooded

c. hominid

d. primitive

The First Primates

2. When did the first primates live?

a. when dinosaurs lived

b. after dinosaurs died out

c. before dinosaurs lived

d. at the beginning of Earth

3. What is the same about all primate eyes?

a. They see in three dimensions.

b. They are on the side.

c. They don't have eyelids.

d. They don't have eyelashes.

4. What is the same about all primate hands?

a. They have an opposable thumb.

b. They have three fingers.

c. They have claws.

d. They are bigger than feet.

Apes and Chimpanzees

Circle the letter of the best answer for each question.

5. What might chimpanzees and humans share?

a. the same ancestor

b. the same size of teeth

c. the same type of fur

d. the same way of walking

Hominids

6. What is one difference between hominids and other primates?

a. Other primates don't have fingers.

b. Other primates don't have eyes.

c. Other primates don't walk upright.

d. Other primates don't share an ancestor.

HOMINIDS THROUGH TIME

7. When is a fossil classified as a hominid?

a. when it is like a human

b. when it is like a primate

c. when it has opposable thumbs

d. when it is a plant-eater

The Earliest Hominids

Read the description. Then, draw a line from the dot next to each description to the matching word.

8. the organisms that the earliest hominids were most like ●

9. the place where the earliest hominid were found ●

a. Africa

b. humans

Australopithecines

Circle the letter of the best answer for each question.

10. What is one way australopithecines were different from apes?

a. They may have used tools.

b. They had hair.

c. They had thumbs.

d. Their eyes were in front.

A Variety of Early Hominids

11. What is one way later hominids were different from australopithecines?

a. They were vegetarians.

b. They had massive teeth.

c. They lived in forests.

d. They built tree houses.

Global Hominids

Read the words in the box. Read the sentences. Fill in the blank with the word or phrase that best completes the sentence.

Homo erectus	*Homo habilis*

12. A hominid that lived two million years ago was

______________________________.

13. A hominid that could grow as tall as modern humans do was

______________________________.

RECENT HOMINIDS

Circle the letter of the best answer for each question.

14. What two types of hominids lived together 30,000 years ago?

a. Neanderthals, *Homo sapiens*

b. australopithecines, others

c. *Homo habilis*, *Homo erectus*

d. monkeys, lemurs

Neanderthals

15. What is one thing Neanderthals did that most humans do today?

a. rode horses

b. ate tough plants

c. buried their dead

d. built temples

16. What happened to the Neanderthals?

a. They disappeared.

b. They are still alive.

c. They moved to Australia.

d. They moved to North America.

Early and Modern Humans

17. How were *Homo sapiens'* faces different from Neanderthals' faces?

a. smaller and flatter

b. more square

c. bigger and hairier

d. long and narrow

Circle the letter of the best answer for each question.

18. What is the only group of hominids still existing?

a. australopithecines

b. *Homo erectus*

c. Neanderthals

d. *Homo sapiens*

19. What was *Homo sapiens* the first hominid to make?

a. houses and fires

b. hunting knives and spears

c. art

d. simple tools

Drawing the Hominid Family Tree

20. Why do scientists keep adding details to their ideas about hominids?

a. More fossils are found.

b. Bushes are discovered.

c. More fossils break.

d. More trees are found.

Name ______________________ Class ______________ Date ____________

Assessment

Chapter Test C

The History of Life on Earth

MULTIPLE CHOICE

Circle the letter of the best answer for each question.

1. What are traces of living things that are preserved in rock called?

a. oxygen

b. fossils

c. sediments

d. dinosaurs

2. What is measuring the age of fossils in years called?

a. relative dating

b. geologic dating

c. absolute dating

d. year dating

3. What are blocks of time in the geological time scale called?

a. centuries

b. eras

c. years

d. days

4. What do scientists think life developed from?

a. simple chemicals

b. oxygen

c. photosynthesis

d. a nucleus

MULTIPLE CHOICE

Circle the letter of the best answer for each question.

5. During the Paleozoic era, where did plants and animals slowly move?

a. into the air

b. onto the land

c. into the oceans

d. into the trees

6. What reptiles of the Mesozoic era are the best known?

a. newts

b. salamanders

c. snakes

d. dinosaurs

7. What kind of animal is the Cenozoic era famous for?

a. reptiles

b. birds

c. mammals

d. fish

8. What is the same about all primate hands?

a. They are large.

b. They have three fingers.

c. They have opposable thumbs.

d. They are small.

MATCHING

Read the description. Then, draw a line from the dot next to each description to the matching word.

9. when a species dies out ●
10. traces of living things found in rock ●
11. theory that Earth's crust is broken into seven large plates that move ●
12. type of primate that walks upright and is like a human ●

a. fossil
b. extinct
c. plate tectonics
d. hominid

---

13. early type of hominid found in Africa ●
14. hominid that grew as tall as humans now ●
15. hominid that first made clothing and art and is still here today ●
16. hominid that hunted large animals but disappeared ●

a. australopithecines
b. *Homo erectus*
c. Neanderthals
d. *Homo sapiens*

FILL-IN-THE-BLANK

Read the words in the box. Read the sentences. Fill in each blank with the word or phrase that best completes the sentence.

Cenozoic	Mesozoic
Precambrian time	Paleozoic

17. The time when life began was the ______________________.

18. The era known as the Age of Reptiles was the ______________________.

19. The name of the ______________________ era means "ancient life."

20. The era that we live in is called the ______________________.

Name ______________________ Class ______________ Date ____________

Skills Worksheet

Directed Reading B

Section: Sorting It All Out

Circle the letter of the best answer for each question.

1. What is the name for placing things into groups based on similar characteristics?

   a. grouping

   b. classification

   c. studying

   d. listing

WHY CLASSIFY?

2. What do scientists learn by classifying living things?

   a. which living thing is strongest

   b. the characteristics of different species

   c. which species has the most members

   d. how species get along

HOW DO SCIENTISTS CLASSIFY ORGANISMS?

3. What two groups did scientists divide living things into long ago?

   a. living and nonliving

   b. large and small

   c. hairy and hairless

   d. plants and animals

4. What do taxonomists do?

   a. only take photographs of animals

   b. only name and photograph living things

   c. describe, classify, and name living things

   d. only take photographs of plants

Classification Today

Circle the letter of the best answer for each question.

5. How many levels of classification do scientists use today?

a. seven

b. six

c. five

d. four

6. What do closely related living things share?

a. size only

b. shape only

c. many characteristics

d. color and size only

7. What characteristics do platypuses, brown bears, lions, and house cats all share?

a. giving birth to live young

b. retractable claws

c. ability to purr

d. hair and mammary glands

Branching Diagrams

8. What do lions and house cats have that brown bears don't have?

a. ability to purr

b. retractable claws

c. hair and mammary glands

d. giving birth to live young

Circle the letter of the best answer for each question.

9. Which of the following pairs of animals are the most closely related?

a. lions and house cats

b. lions and platypuses

c. house cats and platypuses

d. house cats and brown bears

10. What characteristic is shared by bears, lions, and cats?

a. hooves

b. giving birth to live young

c. hair, mammary glands

d. mane and tail

LEVELS OF CLASSIFICATION

Read the words in the box. Read the sentences. Fill in each blank with the word that best completes the sentence.

kingdoms	classes	species	genera

11. The largest, most general groups for classifying organisms are

______________________.

12. Kingdoms are sorted into phyla, and phyla into

______________________.

13. Orders are separated into families, and families are broken down into ______________________.

14. Genera are sorted into ______________________.

SCIENTIFIC NAMES

Circle the letter of the best answer for each question.

15. What kind of name is specific to each living thing?

a. common name

b. nickname

c. scientific name

d. last name

Two-Part Names

16. Which level of classification does the first part of a scientific name come from?

a. order

b. genus

c. kingdom

d. species

17. Which level of classification does the second part of a scientific name come from?

a. order

b. genus

c. kingdom

d. species

18. What is the scientific name for the Asian elephant?

a. *Felis domesticus*

b. *Elephas maximus*

c. *Tyrannosaurus rex*

d. *Canis lupus*

DICHOTOMOUS KEYS

Circle the letter of the best answer for each question.

19. Why do scientists use dichotomous keys?

a. to name organisms

b. to identify organisms

c. to count organisms

d. to catch organisms

20. What do dichotomous keys use to identify organisms?

a. pairs of questions

b. pairs of arrows

c. pairs of statements

d. pairs of illustrations

A GROWING SYSTEM

21. How do scientists classify living things that do not fit into an existing category?

a. leave the living thing alone

b. try to change the living thing

c. destroy the living thing

d. create a new category

22. Which living thing did not fit in any category?

a. *Symbion pandora*

b. *Felis domesticus*

c. *Elephas maximus*

d. *Tyrannosaurus rex*

Name ______________________ Class ______________ Date ______________

Skills Worksheet

Directed Reading B

Section: The Six Kingdoms

Circle the letter of the best answer for each question.

1. What categories did people think all organisms fit into before *Euglena* was discovered?

a. plants or animals

b. fish or birds

c. plants or mammals

d. animals or trees

WHAT IS IT?

2. On what basis do scientists classify organisms?

a. shape

b. size

c. smell

d. characteristics

3. What are some of *Euglena's* plant-like characteristics?

a. single celled, moves around

b. green, tall, has flowers

c. green, makes food

d. moves, eats other organisms

4. What are some of *Euglena's* animal-like characteristics?

a. single-celled, moves around

b. green, tall, has flowers

c. single-celled, green, makes food

d. moves, eats other organisms

Circle the letter of the best answer for each question.

5. What kingdom did scientists add for organisms that have both plant and animal characteristics?

a. *Euglena*

b. Protista

c. Fungi

d. Animalia

6. Today, how many kingdoms do scientists use to classify all living things?

a. five

b. six

c. seven

d. eight

TWO KINGDOMS OF BACTERIA

7. What is the name given to small, single-celled organisms with no nuclei?

a. seeds

b. bacteria

c. *Euglena*

d. germs

8. What are the two bacteria kingdoms?

a. large and small

b. nucleus and no nucleus

c. young and old

d. Archaebacteria and Eubacteria

Archaebacteria

<u>Circle the letter</u> of the best answer for each question.

9. What does the prefix "archae" mean?

a. cold
b. small
c. ancient
d. new

10. What kind of bacteria can live where other organisms cannot survive?

a. Archaebacteria
b. Eubacteria
c. Protista
d. Fungi

Eubacteria

11. In what other place might you find eubacteria besides soil and water?

a. smoke
b. ice
c. inside the human body
d. hot springs

12. What kind of food do eubacteria help us make from milk?

a. ice cream
b. milkshakes
c. cheese
d. yogurt

13. What kind of infection do eubacteria cause in people?

a. bad colds
b. flu
c. pneumonia
d. warts

KINGDOM PROTISTA

Read the words in the box. Read the sentences. Fill in each blank with the word that best completes the sentence.

protists	eukaryotes	protozoans
Euglena	algae	kingdom

14. Organisms that have nuclei and cell membranes are called

______________________.

15. All eukaryotes that are not classified as plants, fungi, or animals are called ______________________.

16. The kingdom Protista contains plant-like organisms called

______________________.

17. The kingdom Protista contains animal-like organisms called

______________________.

18. The kingdom Protista contains organisms that don't fit into any other ______________________.

19. One member of the kingdom Protista is the

______________________.

KINGDOM FUNGI

Circle the letter of the best answer for the question.

20. What can plants do that fungi cannot?

a. cellular respiration

b. fermentation

c. photosynthesis

d. digestion

Circle the letter of the best answer for each question.

21. Which statement about fungi is true?

a. They reproduce using spores.

b. They can move.

c. They eat food.

d. Wild fungi are always safe to eat.

22. Where do fungi get their nutrients?

a. from animals

b. from the sun

c. from their surroundings

d. from energy

23. How do fungi use nutrients?

a. They absorb and digest them.

b. They chew and swallow them.

c. They produce them.

d. They capture and eat them.

KINGDOM PLANTAE

24. What kind of eukaryotic organisms have cell walls and make their own food?

a. animals

b. plants

c. protists

d. fungi

25. Most life on Earth depends on

a. plants.

b. protists.

c. fungi.

d. animals.

26. What must plants be exposed to for photosynthesis to occur?

a. rainwater

b. food

c. sunlight

d. animals

27. What do plants provide for many other organisms?

a. fungi

b. protozoa

c. sunlight

d. a place to live

KINGDOM ANIMALIA

28. What characteristics do most members of kingdom Animalia have?

a. They are unicellular and green.

b. They have cell walls.

c. They are multicellular and can move.

d. They have feathers or hair.

29. What do sense organs allow animals to do?

a. to digest their food

b. to respond to their environment

c. to grow

d. to rest

30. What do animals depend on bacteria and fungi for?

a. to recycle nutrients in the environment

b. to supply chlorophyll

c. to eat

d. to use sunlight

Simple Animals

31. Which of these is an example of a very simple animal that cannot move and has no sense organs?

a. tortoise

b. beetle

c. sponge

d. bird

Name ______________________ Class ______________ Date ____________

Assessment

Chapter Test C

Classification

MULTIPLE CHOICE

Circle the letter of the best answer for each question.

1. What do scientists look at to classify living things?

a. their age

b. their likes and dislikes

c. their characteristics

d. their diseases

2. What is the science of taxonomy?

a. naming plants and animals

b. describing, classifying, and naming living things

c. measuring living things

d. taking pictures of living things

3. In the past, what two groups did scientists use to classify all living things?

a. living and nonliving

b. tall and short

c. plant and animal

d. large and small

4. How many levels of classification do scientists use today?

a. four

b. five

c. six

d. seven

5. How many kingdoms do scientists use to classify living things today?

a. five

b. seven

c. six

d. four

6. What aid can help you identify a living thing you don't know?

a. a dictionary

b. a dichotomous key

c. a photograph

d. taxonomy

Circle the letter of the best answer for each question.

7. What makes up a living thing's scientific name?

a. its genus and species

b. its kingdom and phylum

c. its class and order

d. its family and genus

8. What is the scientific name for an Asian elephant?

a. *Elephas asian*

b. *Elephas maximus*

c. *Elephas biggus*

d. *Elephas rex*

9. What do we call simple, multicellular living things?

a. Protists

b. bacteria

c. Eubacteria

d. Archaebacteria

10. How do fungi take in and use nutrients from their surroundings?

a. They capture and kill them.

b. They chop and swallow them.

c. They absorb and chew them.

d. They absorb and digest them.

11. What must a plant be exposed to for photosynthesis to occur?

a. cold water

b. food

c. sunlight

d. energy

MATCHING

Read the description. Then, draw a line from the dot next to each description to the matching word.

12. They are found where other living things cannot survive. ●

13. They can live in soil, water, or in the human body. ●

14. They are small, single-celled living things without nuclei. ●

a. Eubacteria

b. bacteria

c. Archaebacteria

---

15. They are eukaryotic living things with cell walls that make their own food. ●

16. They can respond quickly to changes in their environment ●

17. Many animals depend on plants for this. ●

a. food

b. plants

c. animals

FILL-IN-THE-BLANK

Read the words in the box. Read the sentences. Fill in each blank with the word that best completes the sentence.

kingdoms	classes	species
genera	orders	

18. The largest, most general groups for classifying organisms are

______________________.

19. Kingdoms are sorted into phyla, and phyla into

______________________.

20. Classes include one or more ______________________.

21. Orders are separated into ______________________.

22. Families are broken down into

______________________.

23. Genera are sorted into ______________________.

Name ______________________ Class ______________ Date ____________

Skills Worksheet

Directed Reading B

Section: Bacteria

Circle the letter of the best answer for each question.

1. What type of living thing are there more of on Earth than all other living things combined?

a. viruses

b. bacteria

c. insects

d. humans

CHARACTERISTICS OF BACTERIA

2. How many kingdoms are used to group living things?

a. one

b. two

c. six

d. ten

3. What kingdoms are made up of bacteria?

a. Eubacteria and Archaebacteria

b. Fungi and Animalia

c. Archaebacteria and Fungi

d. Protista and Plantae

4. What kingdoms contain the oldest forms of life?

a. Fungi and Plantae

b. Eubacteria and Archaebacteria

c. Eubacteria and Protista

d. Animalia and Plantae

Circle the letter of the best answer for each question.

5. How many cells do bacteria have?

a. one

b. two

c. three

d. more than three

The Shape of Bacteria

6. What gives a bacteria its shape?

a. its size

b. the kingdom it belongs to

c. its cell wall

d. its color

Read the description. Then, draw a line from the dot next to each description to the matching word.

7. rod-shaped	**a.** cocci
8. long and spiral-shaped	**b.** bacilli
9. spherical	**c.** spirilla

Read the words in the box. Read the sentences. Fill in each blank with the word or phrase that best completes the sentence.

flagella	eukaryote	nucleus
binary fission	endospore	prokaryote

10. Hairlike parts called ______________________ help bacteria move around.

No Nucleus!

11. Bacteria have one cell and no ______________________.

12. An organism with no nucleus is a(n)

______________________.

13. An organism with a nucleus is a(n) ______________________.

Bacterial Reproduction

14. Reproduction in which a single-celled organism splits into two single-celled organisms is called

______________________.

Endospores

15. Genetic material can exist for millions of years in a thick-walled

______________________.

Kingdom Eubacteria

Circle the letter of the best answer for each question.

16. What are most bacteria?

a. archaebacteria

b. protista

c. fungi

d. eubacteria

Circle the letter of the best answer for each question.

17. What kingdom has the most individuals?

a. Archaebacteria

b. Eubacteria

c. Fungi

d. Protista

Eubacteria Classification

18. How are eubacteria classified?

a. by shape

b. by size

c. by how they get food

d. by how they reproduce

19. What are most eubacteria?

a. consumers

b. producers

c. decomposers

d. food sources

Read the description. Then, draw a line from the dot next to each description to the matching word.

20. bacteria that make their own food

21. bacteria that get their food from dead organic matter

22. bacteria that eat other organisms or live in or on the body of another organism

23. bacteria that contain the green pigment chlorophyll

a. decomposers

b. producers

c. consumers

d. cyanobacteria

KINGDOM ARCHAEBACTERIA

Harsh Environments

24. live in ocean vents and hot springs

25. live in swamps and animal intestines

26. live in salty environments

27. often live where nothing else can

a. methane makers

b. salt lovers

c. archaebacteria

d. heat lovers

Name ______________________ Class ______________ Date ____________

Skills Worksheet

Directed Reading B

Section: Bacteria's Role in the World

Circle the letter of the best answer for each question.

GOOD FOR THE ENVIRONMENT

1. How do bacteria help the environment?

a. keep nitrogen away from plants

b. recycle dead animals and plants

c. cause disease

d. cause cavities

Nitrogen Fixation

2. Where do plants get nitrogen?

a. from air

b. from water

c. from soil

d. from bacteria

3. Why don't plants get nitrogen from the air?

a. There's no nitrogen in air.

b. There's not enough nitrogen in air.

c. It's in a form they can't use.

d. Plants don't need nitrogen to grow.

4. What do bacteria do to nitrogen so plants can use it?

a. change its form

b. absorb it

c. dissolve it

d. increase it

Circle the letter of the best answer for each question.

5. What is the process called where bacteria changes nitrogen into a form plants can use?

   a. nitrogen formation

   b. nitrogen change

   c. nitrogen fixation

   d. nitrogen cycle

Recycling

6. What breaks down dead plant and animal matter?

   a. nitrogen

   b. producer bacteria

   c. consumer bacteria

   d. decomposer bacteria

Cleaning Up

7. Which of the following uses microorganisms to change harmful chemicals into harmless ones?

   a. decomposition

   b. bioremediation

   c. nitrogen fixation

   d. binary fission

GOOD FOR PEOPLE

Bacteria in Your Food

Read the words in the box. Read the sentences. Fill in each blank with the word or phrase that best completes the sentences.

lactose	bacteria	insulin
antibiotics	genetic engineering	

8. Bacteria changes ______________________ into lactic acid, which helps to preserve food.

Making Medicines

9. Medicines used to kill bacteria are ______________________.

10. Many antibiotics are made by ______________________.

Insulin

11. Scientists put genes into a bacterium so they would make ______________________.

Genetic Engineering

12. Changing the genes of bacteria or other living things is called ______________________.

HARMFUL BACTERIA

Circle the letter of the best answer for each questions.

13. What are bacteria that cause disease?

a. pathogenic bacteria
b. host
c. lactic bacteria
d. genetic bacteria

Name ______________________ Class ______________ Date ____________

Directed Reading B *continued*

Circle the letter of the best answer for each questions.

14. How do pathogenic bacteria harm the host organism?

a. take nutrients from its cells

b. take nitrogen from its cells

c. through bioremediation

d. through genetic engineering

15. What protects people from many bacterial diseases?

a. bioremediation

b. childhood vaccinations

c. genetic engineering

d. insulin

16. How are many bacterial diseases treated?

a. bioremediation

b. vaccines

c. genetic engineering

d. antibiotics

Diseases in Other Organisms

17. What do odd-colored spots on a plant show?

a. lack of nitrogen

b. too much nitrogen

c. genetic engineering

d. bacterial damage

18. How are plants treated for bacterial damage?

a. fertilizer

b. antibiotics

c. sunshine

d. cutting

19. How can scientists make plants resistant to disease-causing bacteria?

a. by genetic engineering

b. by changing their soil

c. by increasing their nutrients

d. by moving their location

Name ______________________ Class ______________ Date ____________

Skills Worksheet

Directed Reading B

Section: Viruses

Circle the letter of the best answer for each question.

1. What tiny particle gets inside a cell and often destroys it?

a. virus
b. bacteria
c. nucleus
d. host

2. What do viruses cause?

a. decay
b. bacterial infections
c. cell growth
d. diseases

IT'S A SMALL WORLD

3. How big are viruses?

a. bigger than bacteria
b. smaller than bacteria
c. one inch wide
d. one-quarter inch wide

4. What is a trait of viruses?

a. They can grow very large.
b. They can change quickly.
c. They never change.
d. They change very slowly.

5. What are two traits that make viruses hard to fight?

a. They are too hard to see and too fast.
b. They are too small and change too often.
c. They are too small and too fast.
d. They are too big and too fast.

ARE VIRUSES LIVING?

6. How are viruses like living things?

a. Viruses eat.
b. Viruses break down food.
c. Viruses reproduce.
d. Viruses grow.

Circle the letter of the best answer for each question.

7. How are viruses DIFFERENT from living things?

a. They reproduce.

b. They contain protein.

c. They can't live on their own.

d. They contain genetic material.

8. Where do viruses reproduce?

a. inside a host

b. inside other viruses

c. inside bacteria

d. in the air

9. What is a host?

a. a bacterium

b. a virus

c. a disease

d. a living thing that a virus lives on or in

10. What do viruses force a host to make?

a. new cells

b. viruses

c. bacteria

d. hosts

CLASSIFYING VIRUSES

11. Which is NOT a way of grouping viruses?

a. by shape

b. by size

c. by life cycle

d. by the type of diseases they cause

Read the description. Then, draw a line from the dot next to each description to the matching word.

12. tobacco mosaic virus	**a.** spacecraft
13. HIV and the influenza virus	**b.** spheres
14. viruses that attack only bacteria	**c.** crystals
15. polio virus	**d.** cylinders

---

16. genetic material in cold, flu, and AIDS	**a.** protein coat
17. substance that protects genetic material and helps viruses enter cells	**b.** DNA
18. virus that causes AIDS	**c.** RNA
19. genetic material in warts and chickenpox	**d.** HIV

A DESTRUCTIVE HOUSE GUEST

Read the words in the box. Read the sentences. Fill in each blank with the word or phrase that best completes the sentence.

lysogenic	genetic	lytic
viruses	host	

20. Viruses attack cells and turn them into virus factories in the

______________________ cycle.

21. In the lytic cycle, a virus enters a cell and injects it with the virus's

______________________ material.

22. During the lytic cycle, the genes take over the host and make

______________________.

23. Newly made viruses break out of the

______________________, which then dies.

A Time Bomb

24. In the ______________________ cycle, the virus's genes are inactive for a long period of time.

Treating a Virus

Read the description. Then draw a line from the dot next to each description to the matching word.

25. medicines that do not kill viruses ●

26. procedure that helps prevent viral infections ●

27. type of medicine that keeps viruses from reproducing ●

a. antiviral

b. antibiotics

c. vaccinations

Name ______________________ Class ______________ Date ____________

Assessment

Chapter Test C

Bacteria and Viruses

MULTIPLE CHOICE

Circle the letter of the best answer for each question.

1. How many cells do bacteria have?

a. one

b. two

c. three

d. four or more

2. How do bacteria help the environment?

a. Bacteria keep nitrogen away from plants.

b. Bacteria recycle dead animals and plants.

c. Bacteria cause disease.

d. Bacteria cause cavities.

3. How do viruses reproduce?

a. by means of the lytic cycle

b. by means of the lysogenic cycle

c. by means of the lytic cycle and lysogenic cycle

d. by means of binary fission

4. What organism can live where no other organisms live?

a. archaebacteria

b. eubacteria

c. cyanobacteria

d. viruses

MULTIPLE CHOICE

Circle the letter of the best answer for each question.

5. Which of the following is a shape of bacteria?

a. sphere

b. bacilli

c. oval

d. cylinder

6. Which of the following is a shape of viruses?

a. crystal

b. cocci

c. spirilla

d. bacilli

7. What is one way to prevent viral infections?

a. bioremediation

b. genetic engineering

c. vaccinations

d. antibiotics

8. What is one way viruses are like living things?

a. They eat.

b. They move.

c. They grow.

d. They reproduce.

Name ______________________ Class ______________ Date ____________

MATCHING

Read the description. Then, draw a line from the dot next to each description to the matching word.

9. bacteria that cause disease ●

10. an organism without a nucleus ●

11. a tiny organism that invades a cell and destroys it ●

12. a living thing that a virus lives on or in ●

a. prokaryote

b. virus

c. pathogenic bacteria

d. host

---

13. medicines that kill bacteria ●

14. medicines that keep viruses from reproducing ●

15. changing harmful chemicals to harmless ones ●

16. a way to prevent viral infections ●

a. antivirals

b. antibiotics

c. vaccinations

d. bioremediation

FILL-IN-THE-BLANK

Read the words in the box. Read the sentences. <u>Fill in each blank</u> with the word or phrase that best completes the sentence.

binary fission	endospores	nitrogen fixation	lytic

17. Viruses enter a living cell and use it to make more viruses in the ______________________ cycle.

18. Bacteria reproduce by ______________________.

19. Genetic material from millions of years ago can survive in ______________________.

20. Bacteria change nitrogen into a form plants can use by ______________________.

Name ______________________ Class ______________ Date __________

Skills Worksheet

Directed Reading B

Section: Protists

Circle the letter of the best answer for each question.

1. What kingdom do protists belong to?

a. Plant

b. Animal

c. Protista

d. Fungus

GENERAL CHARACTERISTICS

2. Most protists are made of how many cells?

a. four

b. three

c. two

d. one

3. What term means that protists' cells have a nucleus?

a. eukaryotic

b. nucleusatic

c. chloroplasts

d. microscopic

4. Which of the following statements about protists is NOT true?

a. Some protists live in colonies.

b. Some protists have specialized tissues.

c. Some protists produce their own food.

d. Some protists control their own movement.

5. Which of the following is an example of a protist?

a. witch's hat fungus

b. mold

c. nucleus

d. pretzel slime mold

PROTISTS AND FOOD

Producing Food

Circle the letter of the best answer for each question.

6. What do chloroplasts do?

a. capture energy from the sun

b. give a protist its shape

c. help the protist move

d. help the protist eat other organisms

7. How do some protists make their own food?

a. by decomposition

b. by photogenesis

c. by photosynthesis

d. by heterotrophy

Read the words in the box. Read the sentences. Fill in each blank with the word or phrase that best completes the sentence.

host	parasite	heterotroph

8. An organism that cannot make its own food is called a(n)

_______________________.

9. A protist that invades another living thing to get the nutrients it needs is a(n) _______________________.

10. A living thing that a parasite invades is a(n)

_______________________.

Read the description. Then, draw a line from the dot next to each description to the matching word.

11. a protist that makes its own food ●

12. a heterotroph that gets energy by breaking down dead matter ●

13. the part of a protist that captures energy from the sun ●

a. decomposer

b. producer

c. chloroplast

PRODUCING MORE PROTISTS

Asexual Reproduction

Circle the letter of the best answer for each question.

14. In asexual reproduction, how many parents are there?

a. one

b. two

c. three

d. four

15. What do single-celled protists use to divide into two cells?

a. conjugation

b. binary fission

c. multiple fission

d. single-cell fission

16. What do single-celled protists use to make more than two offspring from one parent?

a. conjugation

b. binary fission

c. multiple fission

d. single-cell fission

Sexual Reproduction

Circle the letter of the best answer for each question.

17. How do paramecium sometimes reproduce?

a. by conjugation

b. by budding

c. by spreading spores

d. by single-cell fission

18. During conjugation, how many new protists are made?

a. one

b. two

c. three

d. four

Read the words in the box. Read the sentences. Fill in each blank with the word or phrase that best completes the sentence.

sexually	malaria	mosquitoes

19. A protist may reproduce ______________________ if there is little food or water.

20. *Plasmodium vivax* causes the disease ______________________.

21. *P. vivax* depends on humans and ______________________ to reproduce.

Name ______________________ Class ______________ Date ____________

Skills Worksheet

Directed Reading B

Section: Kinds of Protists

Circle the letter of the best answer for each question.

1. What is one way protists are grouped?

a. their size

b. their color

c. where they live

d. their shared traits

PROTIST PRODUCERS

2. Which group does NOT include any protists?

a. producers

b. heterotrophs that move

c. heterotrophs that don't move

d. plants

3. All types of algae have what color pigment?

a. red

b. blue

c. brown

d. green

4. Where do most types of algae live?

a. in dirt

b. in water

c. in sand

d. in plants

Circle the letter of the best answer for each question.

5. Which algae live in shallow water along the shore?
   a. phytoplankton
   b. seaweeds
   c. water molds
   d. radiolarians

6. Which of the following provides most of the world's oxygen?
   a. phytoplankton
   b. seaweed
   c. amoebas
   d. flagellates

Read the description. Then, draw a line from the dot next to each description to the matching word.

7. protist producers that use photosynthesis to make food
8. algae that get their color from chlorophyll
9. the algae that include most of the world's seaweeds
10. many single-celled protists living as a group

a. green algae
b. algae
c. colony
d. red algae

---

11. free-floating single-celled algae
12. the algae that include most of the seaweeds in cool climates
13. a green alga that grows in round colonies

a. brown algae
b. *Volvox*
c. phytoplankton

Diatoms

Read the words in the box. Read the sentences. Fill in each blank with the word or phrase that best completes the sentence.

flagella	euglenoids	diatoms

14. Protist producers with a two-part shell are called

______________________________.

Dinoflagellates

15. Dinoflagellates have two whip like strands called

______________________________ that spin them through water.

Euglenoids

16. Because they get food many ways, ______________________________

do not fit well into any group.

HETEROTROPHS THAT CAN MOVE

Circle the letter of the best answer for each question.

17. What are mobile protists sometimes called?

a. protozoans

b. radiolarians

c. foraminiferans

d. paramecium

Amoebas

18. Where are amoebas NOT found?

a. in fresh and salt water

b. in soil

c. in dry sand

d. as parasites in animals

Circle the letter of the best answer for each question.

19. What do most amoebas eat?

a. rocks and soil

b. seaweed

c. plants and bugs

d. bacteria and small protists

Amoebic Movement

20. What does an amoeba use pseudopodia for?

a. eating and moving

b. moving and reproducing

c. reproducing and eating

d. growing and eating

21. What does an amoeba form when it surrounds its food?

a. a contractile vacuole

b. a colony

c. a food vacuole

d. a cilia

Flagellates

Read the description. Then, draw a line from the dot next to each description to the matching word.

22. This is two organisms living closely and each benefiting. ●

23. These have shells that look like glass ornaments. ●

24. These can live in the digestive tract of vertebrates. ●

25. These have snail-like shells. ●

a. foraminiferans

b. radiolarians

c. mutualism

d. *Giardia lamblia*

Ciliates

Read the words in the box. Read the sentences. <u>Fill in each blank</u> with the word or phrase that best completes the sentence.

micronucleus	cilia	macronucleus

26. The tiny, hairlike parts on a ciliate are called

______________________.

27. The nucleus that controls the functions of the cell is called a(n)

______________________.

28. The nucleus that passes genes during reproduction is called a(n)

______________________.

HETEROTROPHS THAT CAN'T MOVE

Spore-Forming Protists

<u>Circle the letter</u> of the best answer for each question.

29. What group do all spore-forming protists belong to?

a. ciliates

b. parasites

c. producers

d. hosts

Water Molds

Circle the letter of the best answer for each question.

30. Which of the following is NOT a host for water molds?

a. plants

b. animals

c. rocks

d. algae

Slime Molds

31. What are spores?

a. eyespots

b. cilia

c. food passageways

d. reproductive cells

Name ______________________ Class ______________ Date ____________

Skills Worksheet

Directed Reading B

Section: Fungi

CHARACTERISTICS OF FUNGI

Circle the letter of the best answer for each question.

1. Which of the following do fungi NOT have?

a. nucleus in each cell

b. chlorophyll

c. rigid cell walls

d. digestive juices

Food for Fungi

2. Where must fungi live?

a. on or near their food supply

b. in the sun

c. far away from their food supply

d. in the sand

3. What is a helpful relationship between a plant and a fungus called?

a. conjugation

b. decomposition

c. mycorrhiza

d. heterotrophic

Making More Fungi

Read the description. Then, draw a line from the dot next to each description to the matching word.

4. small reproductive cells	●	**a.** hyphae
5. the twisted mass that forms when hyphae grow together	●	**b.** mycelium
6. threadlike fungal fibers	●	**c.** spores

KINDS OF FUNGI

Circle the letter of the best answer for each question.

7. How many main groups of fungi are there?

a. one

b. six

c. four

d. twenty

Threadlike Fungi

8. Which type of fungus is shapeless and fuzzy?

a. yeast

b. *Penicillium*

c. mold

d. mushroom

9. Where do most of the threadlike fungi live?

a. in soil

b. in another organism

c. in water

d. in sand

10. What are the spore cases of threadlike fungi called?

a. sacs

b. sporangia

c. spore molds

d. morels

Sac Fungi

Read the words in the box. Read the sentences. Fill in each blank with the word or phrase that best completes the sentence.

acus	budding	sac	yeast

11. The largest group of fungi are the ______________________________ fungi.

12. When sac fungi reproduce sexually, they form a sac called a(n) ______________________________.

13. To make breads, a type of sac fungi called ______________________________ is used.

14. When yeast cells reproduce asexually, they use a process called ______________________________.

Club Fungi

Read the words in the box. Read the sentences. Fill in each blank with the word or phrase that best completes the sentence.

club fungi	basidia	gills

15. Mushrooms belong to a group of fungi called

_______________________________.

16. The clublike structures formed during reproduction are called

_______________________________.

17. The basidia of gill fungi develop in grooves, or

_______________________________.

Imperfect Fungi

Read the description. Then, draw a line from the dot next to each description to the matching word.

18. a fungus that grows outward from wood and forms small shelves ●

19. a poison produced by one imperfect fungus ●

20. a fungus used to make an antibiotic ●

21. all fungi that do not fit in other groups ●

a. bracket fungi

b. aflatoxin

c. *Penicillium*

d. imperfect fungi

Lichens

Circle the letter of the best answer for each question.

22. A lichen is a combination of what two organisms?

a. fungus and alga

b. alga and yeast

c. fungus and mushroom

d. yeast and mushroom

23. Which of the following groups do lichens belong to?

a. consumers

b. parasites

c. producers

d. hosts

24. What helps to keep water inside lichens?

a. protective walls

b. basidia

c. bacteria

d. spores

25. Besides air and light, what else do lichens need to grow?

a. yeasts

b. minerals

c. bacteria

d. spores

26. What easily affects lichens?

a. darkness

b. dampness

c. dryness

d. air pollution

Name ______________________ Class ______________ Date ____________

Assessment

Chapter Test C

Protists and Fungi

MULTIPLE CHOICE

Circle the letter of the best answer for each question.

1. Most protists are made of how many cells?

a. four

b. three

c. two

d. one

2. What term means that protists' cells have a nucleus?

a. eukaryotic

b. nucleusatic

c. chloroplasts

d. microscopic

3. How do protists make their own food?

a. by decomposition

b. by photogenesis

c. by photosynthesis

d. by conjugation

4. In asexual reproduction, how many parents are there?

a. one

b. two

c. three

d. four

5. What is one way protists are grouped?

a. by their size

b. by their color

c. by where they live

d. by their shared traits

Circle the letter of the best answer for each question.

6. Where do most types of algae live?

a. in dirt

b. in water

c. in sand

d. in plants

7. What are mobile protists sometimes called?

a. protozoans

b. radiolarians

c. foraminiferans

d. paramecia

8. What are the spore cases on threadlike fungi called?

a. sacs

b. sporangia

c. spore mold

d. morels

9. A lichen combines what two organisms?

a. fungus and alga

b. alga and yeast

c. fungus and mushroom

d. yeast and mushroom

10. What is the largest group of fungi?

a. sac fungi

b. imperfect fungi

c. club fungi

d. lichens

MATCHING

Read the description. Then, draw a line from the dot next to each description to the matching word.

11. a protist that makes its own food ●

12. an organism that CANNOT make its own food ●

13. a protist that gets the nutrients it needs from another protist ●

14. a part of a protist that captures energy from the sun ●

a. parasite

b. producer

c. chloroplast

d. heterotroph

---

15. protist producers that use photosynthesis to make food ●

16. a twisted mass that forms when hyphae grow together ●

17. a threadlike fungal fiber ●

18. heterotrophs with rigid cell walls and no chlorophyll ●

a. hypha

b. fungi

c. mycelium

d. algae

FILL-IN-THE-BLANK

Read the words in the box. Read the sentences. Fill in the blank with the word or phrase that best completes the sentence.

decomposers	phytoplankton	mold

19. Heterotrophs that get energy by breaking down dead matter are called ______________________.

20. Free-floating, single-celled algae are called ______________________.

21. A shapeless, fuzzy fungus is called a(n) ______________________.

Name ______________________ Class ______________ Date ____________

Skills Worksheet

Directed Reading B

Section: What Is a Plant?

PLANT CHARACTERISTICS

Photosynthesis

Circle the letter of the best answer for each question.

1. What makes plants green and captures energy from the sun?

a. organelles
b. chlorophyll
c. carbon dioxide
d. chloroplasts

2. What process do plants use to make food?

a. chloroplast
b. organelle
c. photosynthesis
d. producer

Cuticles

3. What is the name of the waxy layer that keeps plants from drying out?

a. cell wall
b. cell membrane
c. photosynthesis
d. cuticle

Cell Walls

4. What helps make cell walls hard?

a. cell membranes and chloroplasts
b. cuticles and photosynthesis
c. carbohydrates and proteins
d. gymnosperms and chlorophyll

5. What lies beneath the cell wall?

a. angiosperm
b. protein
c. cell membrane
d. green algae

Draw a line from each term to the matching number on the picture.

cell wall   vacuole   cell membrane   chloroplast

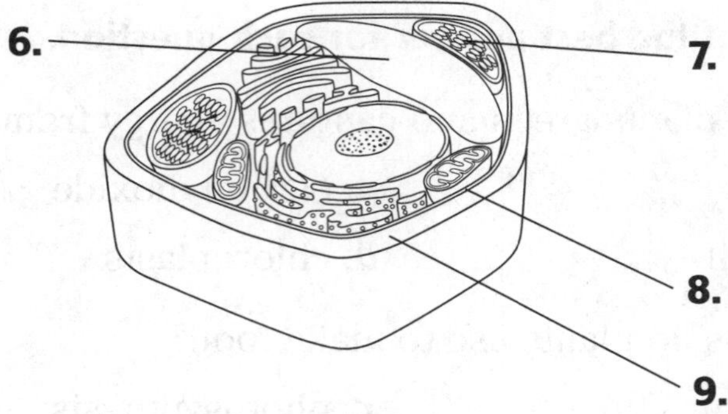

Reproduction

Circle the letter of the best answer for each question.

10. Which of the following is produced during the sporophyte stage?

a. sperm

b. eggs

c. spores

d. sex cells

11. What does a fertilized egg grow into?

a. sporophyte

b. sex cells

c. gametophyte

d. spores

PLANT CLASSIFICATION

Read the description. Then, draw a line from the dot next to each description to the matching word.

12. is a flowering seed plant

13. does not have tissues for moving water and nutrients

14. is a vascular plant that has no flowers

15. has specialized tissues for moving water and nutrients

a. gymnosperm

b. vascular plant

c. angiosperm

d. nonvascular plant

---

16. has seeds but no flowers

17. has vascular tissue but has no seeds

18. has both flowers and seeds

a. seedless vascular plant

b. angiosperm

c. gymnosperm

THE ORIGIN OF PLANTS

Read the words in the box. Read the sentences. Fill in each blank with the word or phrase that best completes the sentence.

ancestor	cell walls
photosynthesis	plant

19. Green algae is not a(n) ______________________.

20. Green algae and plants have ______________________ that are a lot alike.

21. Green algae and plants might share a common ______________________.

22. Green algae and plants both make food through ______________________.

Name ______________________ Class ______________ Date ____________

Skills Worksheet

Directed Reading B

Section: Seedless Plants

Circle the letter of the best answer for each question.

1. What are the two groups of seedless plants?
   - **a.** gymnosperms and angiosperms
   - **b.** rhizoids and rhizomes
   - **c.** seedless vascular plants and nonvascular plants
   - **d.** gametophytes and sporophytes

NONVASCULAR PLANTS

2. Where do nonvascular plants usually live?
   - **a.** dry places
   - **b.** damp places
   - **c.** secret places
   - **d.** cold places

Mosses

3. What helps mosses get water and nutrients?
   - **a.** gametophytes
   - **b.** rhizoids
   - **c.** spores
   - **d.** sunlight

4. During the moss life cycle, what structure releases spores?
   - **a.** fertilized egg
   - **b.** gametophyte
   - **c.** sporophyte
   - **d.** sperm

Circle the letter of the best answer for each question.

5. During the moss life cycle, what do spores grow into?

a. fertilizer

b. gametophytes

c. sporophytes

d. spores

6. What are the two stages of the moss life cycle called?

a. egg and sperm

b. gametophyte and sporophyte

c. swimming and fertilizing

d. air and water

Liverworts and Hornworts

7. What do the gametophytes of hornworts look like?

a. leafy and mosslike

b. rhizoids

c. broad and flattened

d. mosses

The Importance of Nonvascular Plants

8. How do nonvascular plants help the soil?

a. reduce soil erosion

b. keep the soil warm

c. keep the soil wet

d. make the soil thin

Circle the letter of the best answer for each question.

9. How do animals use nonvascular plants?

a. for fuel

b. for food and nesting material

c. in potting soil

d. for water

10. What can dried peat moss be used for?

a. fuel

b. erosion

c. new plants

d. seeds

SEEDLESS VASCULAR PLANTS

Ferns

Read the description. Then, draw a line from the dot next to each description to the matching word.

11. an underground stem	●	**a.** fronds
12. fern leaves	●	**b.** fern gametophyte
13. young frond	●	**c.** fiddlehead
14. smaller than a fingernail	●	**d.** rhizome

Horsetails and Club Mosses

Read the words in the box. Read the sentences. Fill in each blank with the word or phrase that best completes the sentence.

silica	mosses
stems	club mosses

15. Horsetails feel gritty because of ______________________.

16. Silica is found in the ______________________ of horsetails.

17. Plants that are about 20 cm tall and grow in woodlands are called ______________________.

18. Club mosses are not actually ______________________.

The Importance of Seedless Vascular Plants

Circle the letter of the best answer for each question.

19. How do ferns, horsetails, and club mosses help the environment?

a. form soil

b. make silica

c. decrease soil depth

d. create forests

20. What can horsetails be used for?

a. shampoo

b. iron smelting

c. clothing

d. transportation

21. What fuel was formed by seedless plants that died 300 million years ago?

a. nuclear fuel

b. coal

c. hydrogen

d. water

Name ______________________ Class ______________ Date ____________

Skills Worksheet

Directed Reading B

Section: Seed Plants

Circle the letter of the best answer for each question.

1. What types of plants produce seeds?

a. gymnosperms and angiosperms

b. ferns and horsetails

c. nonvascular plants

d. mosses and liverworts

CHARACTERISTICS OF SEED PLANTS

2. How many stages are in the life cycle of a seed plant?

a. one

b. two

c. three

d. four

3. Which of the following does not live independently in seed plants?

a. stems

b. young sporophytes

c. gametophytes

d. young leaves

4. What do the sperm of seedless plants need to reach the eggs?

a. water

b. wind

c. pollen

d. birds

5. Inside what structure do the sperm of seed plants form?

a. water

b. pollen

c. stems

d. seeds

Circle the letter of the best answer for each question.

6. What are the most common plants on Earth?

a. ferns

b. seedless plants

c. sporophytes

d. seed plants

THE STRUCTURE OF SEEDS

Circle the letter of the best answer for each question.

7. What is an advantage of seeds over spores?

a. Food is stored in the seed.

b. Animals leave seeds alone.

c. Seeds grow in damp places.

d. Seeds stay in one place.

Read the description. Then draw a line from the dot next to each description to the matching word.

8. food storage	●	**a.** animals
9. joining of a sperm and an egg	●	**b.** cotyledons
10. can help spread seeds	●	**c.** sporophyte
11. a young plant in a seed	●	**d.** fertilization

GYMNOSPERMS

12. What are seed plants that do NOT have flowers or fruit called?

a. ferns

b. sporophytes

c. spores

d. gymnosperms

Circle the letter of the best answer for each question.

The Importance of Gymnosperms

13. Which of the following is NOT a human use for gymnosperms?

a. building materials

b. a source of resin

c. anticancer drugs

d. food

Read the description. Then, draw a line from the dot next to each description to the matching word.

14. most economically important gymnosperm

15. sticky fluid used in paint

16. produces anticancer drug

17. produces anti-allergy drug

a. resin

b. yew

c. conifers

d. gnetophyte

Gymnosperm Life Cycle

Use the figure below to answer questions 18 through 21. For each question, circle the letter of the best answer for each question.

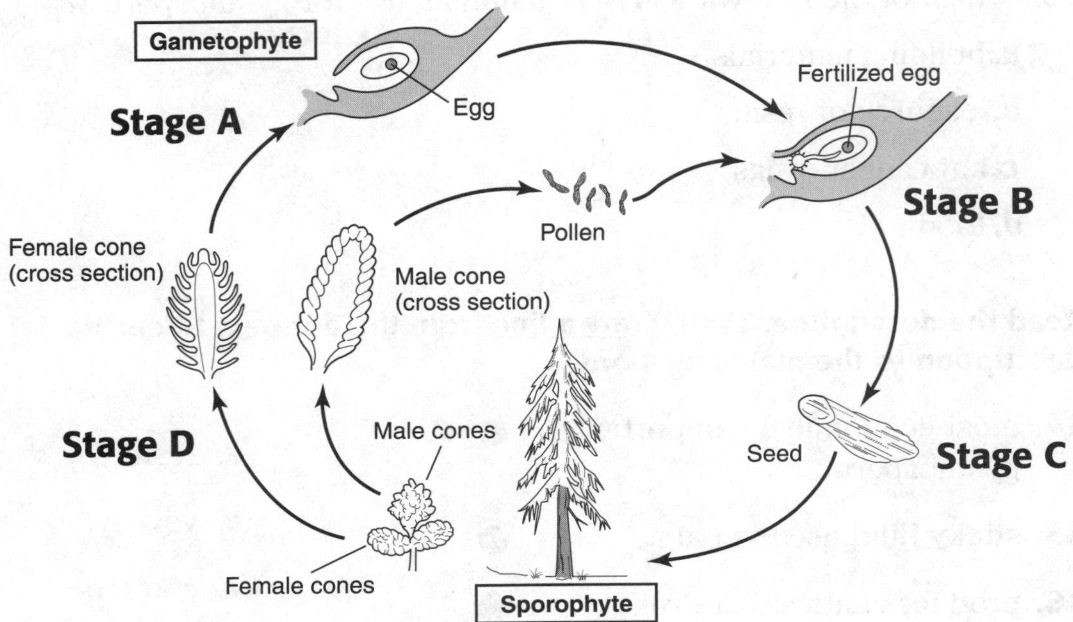

18. At which stage does fertilization occur?

a. Stage A　**c.** Stage C

b. Stage B　**d.** Stage D

19. At which stage are sex cells produced?

a. Stage A　**c.** Stage C

b. Stage B　**d.** Stage D

20. At which stage does the fertilized egg develop into a young sporophyte?

a. Stage A　**c.** Stage C

b. Stage B　**d.** Stage D

21. At which stage are spores produced?

a. Stage A　**c.** Stage C

b. Stage B　**d.** Stage D

Circle the letter of the best answer for each question.

22. Where are sperm found?

a. in pollen
b. in eggs
c. in young sporophytes
d. in rhizoids

ANGIOSPERMS

23. What kind of plants have flowers and fruit?

a. gymnosperms
b. angiosperms
c. ferns
d. mosses

Angiosperm Reproduction

Read the words in the box. Read the sentences. Fill in each blank with the word or phrase that best completes the sentence.

wind	fruit	pollen
flowers	fur	seeds

24. Some animals are attracted to ______________________.

25. Animals may carry ______________________ from flower to flower.

26. Angiosperm seeds are surrounded and protected by ______________________.

27. Some fruits and seeds are blown away by the ______________________.

28. Some animals eat fruit and get rid of the ______________________.

29. Burrs are fruits that stick to the ______________________ of animals.

Name ________________ Class ________ Date ________

Two Kinds of Angiosperms

Read the words in the box. Read the sentences. Fill in each blank with the word or phrase that best completes the sentence.

monocot	dicot

30. There is one seed leaf in a ______________________ seed.

31. There are two seed leaves in a ______________________ seed.

The Importance of Angiosperms

Read the description. Then draw a line from the dot next to each description to the matching word.

32. flowering plant used for building material ●

33. flowering plant used to make clothing ●

34. flowering plant grown for food ●

a. corn

b. oak tree

c. cotton

Name ______________________ Class ______________ Date ______________

Skills Worksheet

Directed Reading B

Section: Structures of Seed Plants

Circle the letter of the best answer for each question.

1. What moves water and minerals through a plant?

a. xylem
b. phloem
c. seeds
d. rhizomes

2. What moves food to all plant parts?

a. xylem
b. phloem
c. seeds
d. rhizomes

ROOTS

3. Where are most roots found?

a. above ground
b. in water
c. underground
d. in seeds

Root Functions

4. What do roots supply for a plant?

a. protection
b. sunlight
c. water and minerals
d. xylem and phloem

5. What holds plants in the soil?

a. stems
b. roots
c. xylem
d. phloem

6. Which of the following is a function of roots?

a. They store food.
b. They get rid of extra water.
c. They capture energy from the sun.
d. They release minerals.

Root Structure

Circle the letter of the best answer for each question.

7. What are the cells covering a root called?

a. root cap
b. stem
c. epidermis
d. root hairs

8. What helps roots get more water?

a. root tip
b. stem
c. root hairs
d. root cap

9. What does the root cap protect?

a. stem
b. food supply
c. root hairs
d. root tip

10. What part of the root produces a slimy substance?

a. root hairs
b. root tip
c. root cap
d. xylem

Root Systems

11. What is a root system with one main root called?

a. root stem
b. root cap
c. taproot
d. fibrous root

12. What is the name of a root system with several roots that are usually the same size?

a. root stem
b. root cap
c. taproot
d. fibrous root

STEMS

Stem Functions

13. Where are most stems found?

a. in roots
b. underground
c. in water
d. above ground

Read the words in the box. Read the sentences. Fill in each blank with the word or phrase that best completes the sentence.

water	support
shoots	roots

14. Stems ______________________ the plant.

15. Stems connect a plant's ______________________ to its leaves.

16. Stems move materials between the roots and ______________________.

17. Some stems store ______________________.

Herbaceous Stems

Circle the letter of the best answer for each question.

18. What are stems that are soft, thin, and flexible called?

a. xylem

b. phloem

c. herbaceous stems

d. woody stems

19. Which of the following has a herbaceous stem?

a. bean plant

b. shrub

c. oak tree

d. pine tree

Woody Stems

Circle the letter of the best answer for each question.

20. What are rigid stems made of wood and bark called?

a. xylen

b. phloem

c. herbaceous stems

d. woody stems

21. What is the name of a ring of dark cells surrounding a ring of light cells in a woody stem?

a. wood ring

b. cross section

c. growth ring

d. stem

LEAVES

22. What size and shape are leaves?

a. many shapes and sizes

b. small and heart-shaped

c. round and large

d. fan-shaped and large

Leaf Functions

Read the description. Then, draw a line from the dot next to each description to the matching word.

23. captures energy from sunlight ●	**a.** food
24. leaves get this from air ●	**b.** carbon dioxide
25. made from carbon dioxide and water ●	**c.** chloroplast

Leaf Structure

Read the description. Then, draw a line from the dot next to each description to the matching word.

26. under the cuticle ●	**a.** guard cell
27. tiny opening that lets carbon dioxide enter the leaf ●	**b.** cuticle
28. stops water loss from a leaf ●	**c.** stomata
29. open and close the stomata ●	**d.** epidermis

Leaf Adaptations

30. modified leaves of cactus ●	**a.** insects
31. has leaves modified to catch insects ●	**b.** sundew
32. where a sundew gets nitrogen ●	**c.** spines

FLOWERS

Circle the letter of the best answer for each question.

33. Why do some plants have flowers?

a. to attract animals
b. to look pretty
c. to keep animals away
d. to attract wind

Sepals and Petals

34. What protects flower buds?

a. sepals
b. petals
c. roots
d. seeds

35. What parts of the flower are broad, leaflike, and attract animals?

a. sepals
b. petals
c. roots
d. seeds

Stamens and Pistils

Read the words in the box. Read the sentences. Fill in each blank with the word or phrase that best completes the sentence.

stamen	ovary	pistil

36. The stigma, style, and ovary are parts of the ______________________.

37. A fruit develops from the ______________________.

38. The filament and anther are parts of the ______________________.

Circle the letter of the best answer for each question.

39. What is the male part of a flower called?

a. pistil

b. ovule

c. style

d. stamen

40. What is the female part of a flower called?

a. pistil

b. filament

c. anther

d. stamen

41. What part of a flower contains the ovules?

a. pistil

b. stamen

c. ovary

d. filament

The Importance of Flowers

Read the words in the box. Read the sentences. Fill in each blank with the word or phrase that best completes the sentence.

cloves	broccoli	chamomile

42. One flower that can be eaten is ______________________.

43. One flower that can be used to make tea is

______________________.

44. One flower that can be used as a spice is

______________________.

Name ______________________ Class ______________ Date ____________

Assessment

Chapter Test C

Introduction to Plants

MULTIPLE CHOICE

Circle the letter of the best answer for each question.

1. What plants get water and nutrients from rhizoids?

a. mosses

b. conifers

c. buttercups

d. angiosperms

2. What plant cell part captures energy from the sun to make food?

a. chloroplasts

b. cell walls

c. cell membranes

d. vacuoles

3. What do the sperm of seedless plants need to reach the eggs?

a. water

b. wind

c. pollen

d. birds

4. What does xylem do?

a. carries food

b. dissolves minerals and food

c. carries water and minerals

d. grows longer roots

MULTIPLE CHOICE

<u>Circle the letter</u> of the best answer for each question.

5. What is the male part of a flower called?

a. pistil

b. ovule

c. style

d. stamen

6. What is the female part of a flower called?

a. pistil

b. filament

c. anther

d. stamen

7. What part of a flower contains the ovules?

a. pistil

b. stamen

c. ovary

d. filament

MATCHING

Read the description. Then, <u>draw a line</u> from the dot next to each description to the matching word.

8. seed plants that do not flower	●	**a.** cuticle
9. holds nonvascular plants in place	●	**b.** cotyledon
10. often stores food	●	**c.** gymnosperm
11. helps stop water loss from a leaf	●	**d.** rhizoids

12. young fern frond	●	**e.** growth rings
13. stems that bend easily	●	**f.** fiddlehead
14. can be used to estimate the age of a tree	●	**g.** nonvascular plant
15. does not have true roots, stems, and leaves	●	**h.** herbaceous

FILL-IN-THE-BLANK

Read the words in the box. Read the sentences. Fill in each blank with the word or phrase that best completes the sentence.

rhizome	fibrous root	stamen
angiosperm	green algae	monocot

16. Plants and ______________________ might share a common ancestor.

17. An underground stem from which new leaves and roots grow is a(n) ______________________.

18. A vascular plant that has flowers and fruit is called a(n) ______________________.

19. A plant seed with one seed leaf is a(n) ______________________.

20. The filament and anther are parts of the ______________________.

21. A root system with many roots of a similar size is called a(n) ______________________ system.

Name ______________________ Class ______________ Date ____________

Skills Worksheet

Directed Reading B

Section: Photosynthesis

Circle the letter of the best answer for each question.

1. Which gas is needed most by plants?

a. oxygen

b. nitrogen

c. carbon dioxide

d. other gases

2. What is the process by which plants make their own food?

a. sugar

b. glucose

c. carbon dioxide

d. photosynthesis

CAPTURING LIGHT ENERGY

3. What is the green pigment in plants called?

a. grana

b. chloroplast

c. chlorophyll

d. cell

4. Why are most plants green?

a. Chlorophyll reflects more wavelengths of green light than those of other colors.

b. The cell walls of plant cells are green.

c. Plants produce green pigments during photosynthesis.

d. Plants are green because of warm weather.

Draw a line from each term to the matching number on the picture.

chloroplast grana

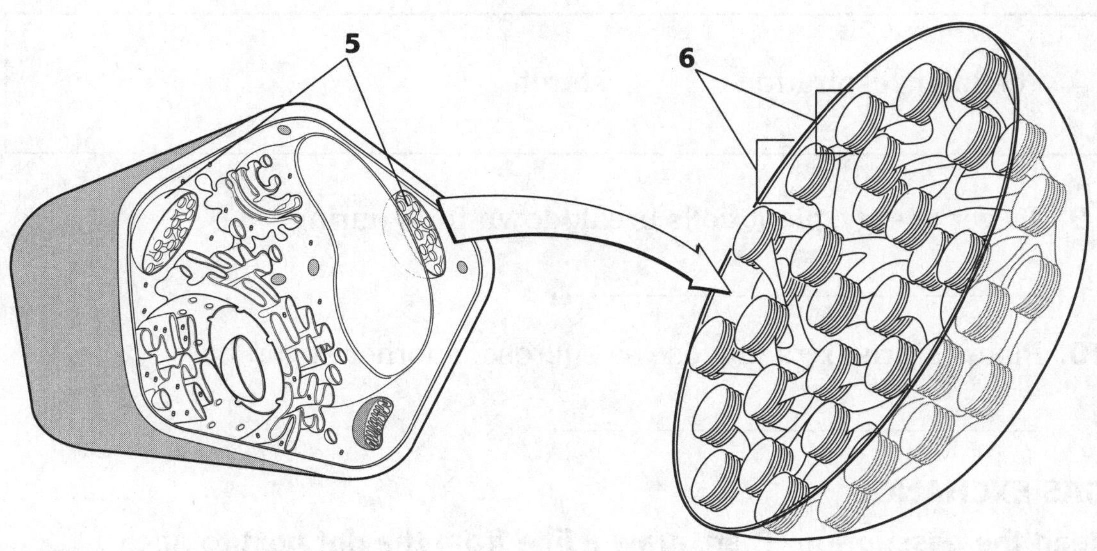

MAKING SUGAR

Read the words in the box. Read the sentences. Fill in each blank with the word or phrase that best completes the sentence.

glucose	oxygen

7. The light energy captured by chlorophyll is used during photosynthesis to produce ______________________.

8. The gas given off during photosynthesis is ______________________.

Name ______________________ Class ______________ Date ____________

GETTING ENERGY FROM SUGAR

Read the words in the box. Read the sentences. Fill in each blank with the word or phrase that best completes the sentence.

cellular respiration	starch

9. To get energy, plant cells break down food during

______________________________.

10. Plants store extra glucose as sucrose, another sugar, or

______________________________.

GAS EXCHANGE

Read the description. Then, draw a line from the dot next to each description to the matching word.

11. a waxy coating that protects the plant from water loss ●

12. an opening in a leaf's epidermis and cuticle ●

13. open and close the stoma ●

14. the loss of water from leaves ●

a. stoma

b. transpiration

c. cuticle

d. guard cells

THE IMPORTANCE OF PHOTOSYNTHESIS

Circle the letter of the best answer for the question.

15. Which of the following forms the base of nearly all food chains on Earth?

a. cellular respiration

b. chlorophyll

c. photosynthetic organisms

d. light energy

Circle the letter of the best answer for each question.

16. What happens during photosynthesis?

a. Plants store light energy as chemical energy.

b. Plants lose their leaves.

c. Plants store chemical energy as light energy.

d. Plants often die.

17. Which of the following is a byproduct of photosynthesis?

a. nitrogen

b. oxygen

c. helium

d. hydrogen

Name ______________________ Class ______________ Date ____________

Skills Worksheet

Directed Reading B

Section: Reproduction of Flowering Plants

FERTILIZATION

Read the words in the box. Read the sentences. Fill in each blank with the word or phrase that best completes the sentence.

pollination	fertilization

1. The movement of pollen from anthers to stigmas is called ______________________.

2. The fusing of sperm with the egg in an ovule is called ______________________.

Use the figure below to answer questions 3 through 6. Read the description. Then, draw a line from the dot next to each description to the matching plant part letter.

3. stigma ●
4. anther ●
5. pollen ●
6. style ●

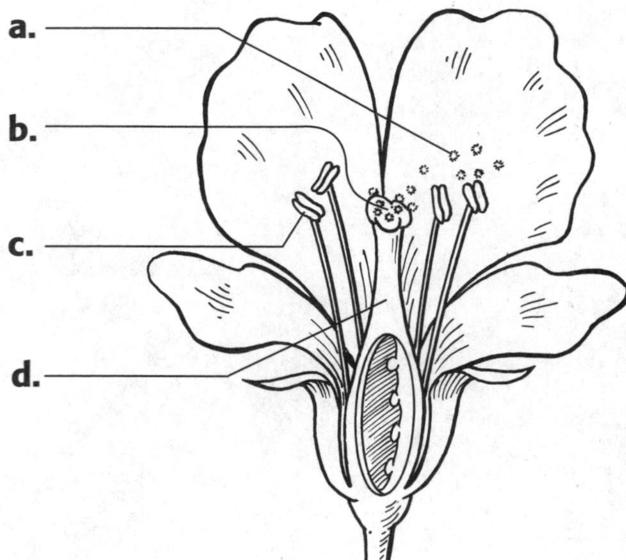

Use the figure below to answer questions 7 through 10. Read the description. Then, draw a line from the dot next to each description to the matching plant part letter.

7. ovary ●

8. sperm ●

9. ovule containing egg ●

10. pollen tube ●

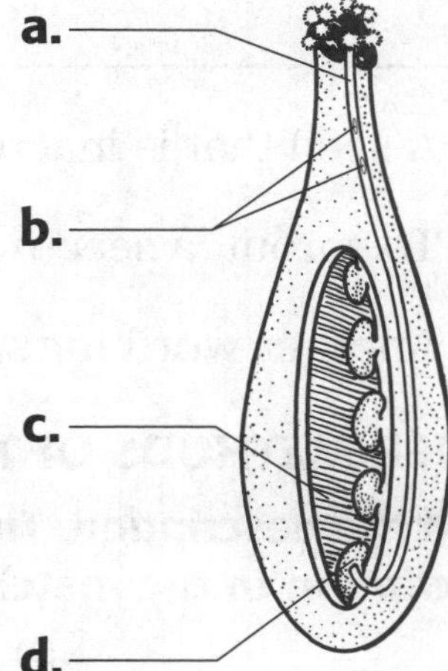

FROM FLOWER TO FRUIT

Read the words in the box. Read the sentences. Fill in each blank with the word that best completes the sentence.

ovule	ovary

11. After fertilization, a seed forms from the

______________________________.

12. After fertilization, a fruit forms from the

______________________________.

FROM SEED TO PLANT

Read the words in the box. Read the sentences. Fill in each blank with the word or phrase that best completes the sentence.

dormant	germination	water, air, and warmth

13. A seed that is inactive is ______________________________.

14. To sprout, a seed needs ______________________________.

15. Another word for sprouting is ______________________________.

OTHER METHODS OF REPRODUCTION

Read the description. Then, draw a line from the dot next to each description to the matching word.

16. above-ground stems from which new plants can grow. ●

17. tiny plants that grow on the edges of leaves and that grow on their own when they fall off ●

18. underground stems that can produce new plants after a dormant season ●

a. plantlets

b. tubers

c. runners

Name ______________________ Class ______________ Date ____________

Skills Worksheet

Directed Reading B

Section: Plant Responses to the Environment

PLANT TROPISMS

Read the words in the box. Read the sentences. Fill in each blank with the word or phrase that best completes the sentence.

tropism	positive tropism	negative tropism

1. Plant growth toward a stimulus is called a

______________________________.

2. Plant growth away from a stimulus is a

______________________________.

3. Plant growth in response to a stimulus is a

______________________________.

Light

Read the description. Then draw a line from the dot next to each description to the matching word.

4. change in direction of plant toward the light ●

5. change in direction of plant either toward or away from the light ●

a. phototropism

b. positive tropism

Gravity

6. change in the direction a plant grows caused by gravity ●

7. change in the growth of a plant's roots toward the center of Earth, or the force of gravity ●

a. positive gravitropism

b. gravitropism

SEASONAL RESPONSES

Length of Day

Read the words in the box. Read the sentences. Fill in each blank with the word or phrase that best completes the sentence.

short-day plants	long-day plants

8. Plants that flower when night length is long are called

______________________________.

9. Plants that flower when night length is short are called

______________________________.

Seasons and Leaf Loss

Read the description. Then draw a line from the dot next to each description to the matching word.

10. type of tree that loses all of its leaves around the same time each year ●

11. type of tree that keeps its leaves year round ●

a. evergreen tree

b. deciduous tree

Seasons and Leaf Color

Read the words in the box. Read the sentences. <u>Fill in each blank</u> with the word or phrase that best completes the sentence.

change color	breaks down	show through

12. Before falling off, leaves of deciduous trees may

______________________________.

13. In fall, green chlorophyll in leaves ______________________________.

14. Without chlorophyll, orange or yellow pigments in leaves

______________________________.

Name ______________________ Class ______________ Date ____________

Assessment

Chapter Test C

Plant Processes

MULTIPLE CHOICE

Circle the letter of the best answer for each question.

1. By which process do plants make their own food from carbon dioxide and water?

a. cellular respiration

b. transpiration

c. chlorophyll

d. photosynthesis

2. Why are many plants green?

a. Plant cells are green.

b. Plants absorb green light.

c. Chlorophyll reflects green light.

d. Rigid cell walls are green.

3. What gas do plants take in to make food?

a. natural gas

b. oxygen

c. carbon dioxide

d. oxygen and carbon dioxide

4. What is the green pigment in plants called?

a. chloroplast

b. chlorophyll

c. photosynthesis

d. grana

MATCHING

Read the description. Then, draw a line from the dot next to each description to the matching word.

5. plants that keep some of their leaves year-round ●
6. plants that bloom when nights are short ●
7. plant growth in response to light or gravity ●
8. trees that lose all of their leaves at about the same time each year ●

a. long-day
b. deciduous
c. evergreen
d. tropism

---

9. sprouting ●
10. tiny plants that grow along the edges of a leaf ●
11. above-ground stems from which new plants can grow ●
12. underground stems from which new plants can grow ●

a. runners
b. tubers
c. plantlets
d. germination

MATCHING

Read the description. Then, draw a line from the dot next to each description to the matching word.

13. process by which plants lose water vapor ●

14. opening in a leaf through which gases can pass ●

15. structure through which sperm travel to reach an ovule ●

16. happens when pollen is moved from the anthers to the stigma ●

a. pollen tube

b. transpiration

c. stoma

d. pollination

FILL-IN-THE-BLANK

Read the words in the box. Read the sentences. Fill in each blank with the word or phrase that best completes the sentence.

ovule	ovary
fertilization	dormant

17. The joining of egg and sperm in an ovule is called ______________________.

18. An inactive seed is ______________________.

19. A seed forms from the ______________________ after fertilization

20. A fruit forms from the ______________________ after fertilization

Name ______________________ Class ______________ Date ____________

Skills Worksheet

Directed Reading B

Section: What Is an Animal?

Circle the letter of the best answer for each question.

1. What are natural bath sponges made of?

a. the remains of plants

b. the remains of animals

c. volcanic rocks

d. sea grass

ANIMAL DIVERSITY

2. How many animals have scientists named?

a. more than 3 million species

b. fewer than 5,000 species

c. fewer than 500,000 species

d. more than 1 million species

Vertebrates

3. What is an animal with a backbone called?

a. invertebrate

b. jellyfish

c. vertebrate

d. sponge

4. How many animal species are vertebrates?

a. about 10%

b. less than 5%

c. about 25%

d. more than 30%

Circle the letter of the best answer for each question.

5. Which of these animals is a vertebrate?

a. worms

b. birds

c. beetles

d. bees

Invertebrates

6. What is an animal with no backbone called?

a. invertebrate

b. mammal

c. vertebrate

d. reptile

7. How many animal species are beetles?

a. about 10%

b. less than 5%

c. about 25%

d. more than 30%

8. Which of these animals is an invertebrate?

a. reptiles

b. birds

c. humans

d. beetles

ANIMAL CHARACTERISTICS

Multicellular Makeup

Read the words in the box. Read the sentences. Fill in each blank with the word or phrase that best completes the sentence.

cell walls	eukaryotic
multicellular	cell membranes

9. All animals are ________________________, which means they are made of many cells.

10. Animal cells are ________________________, which means that they have a nucleus.

11. Unlike plant cells, animal cells do NOT have ________________________.

12. Animal cells are surrounded only by ________________________.

Reproduction and Development

Circle the letter of the best answer for each question.

13. How do almost all animals reproduce?

a. asexually

b. sexually

c. by budding

d. using tissues

14. What are eggs and sperm called?

a. consumers

b. embryos

c. sex cells

d. tissues

Circle the letter of the best answer for each question.

15. What is an organism at an early stage of development called?

a. a tissue

b. a eukaryote

c. a bud

d. an embryo

16. What is it called when part of an organism breaks off and develops a new organism?

a. sexual reproduction

b. an embryo

c. budding

d. a consumer

17. Which of these is an example of an animal that reproduces asexually?

a. beetles

b. hydra

c. sharks

d. mice

Many Specialized Parts

18. When a fertilized egg divides into many cells to become an embryo, what happens to the cells?

a. The cells get smaller.

b. The cells all remain identical.

c. The cells become different from each other.

d. The cells get larger.

Circle the letter of the best answer for each question.

19. What are collections of cells called?

a. buds

b. embryos

c. organs

d. tissues

20. What is a group of tissues that carries out a special function of the body called?

a. an organ

b. a tissue

c. an embryo

d. a consumer

Movement

21. What ability allows animals to search for food, shelter, and mates?

a. estivation

b. consuming

c. movement

d. budding

Consuming

22. What is an organism that eats other organisms called?

a. consumer

b. prey

c. vertebrate

d. invertebrate

Name ______________________ Class ______________ Date ____________

Skills Worksheet

Directed Reading B

Section: Animal Behavior

KINDS OF BEHAVIOR

Read the words in the box. Read the sentences. Fill in each blank with the word or phrase that best completes the sentence.

genes	flying	
innate	walking	learned

1. Behavior that doesn't depend on learning or experience is called ______________________ behavior.

2. Innate behaviors are inherited through ______________________.

3. Behavior that has been learned from experience or from observing other animals is called ______________________ behavior.

4. For bees, ______________________ is an innate behavior that is present at birth.

5. For humans, ______________________ is an innate behavior that takes about one year to develop.

SURVIVAL BEHAVIOR

Finding Food

Read the words in the box. Read the sentences. Fill in each blank with the word or phrase that best completes the sentence.

predators	territory
food and water	prey

6. To survive, an animal must find ______________________.

7. Animals that eat other animals are called

______________________.

8. Animals that are eaten by other animals are

called ______________________.

9. A ______________________ is an area that is occupied by

an animal or a group of animals.

Marking Territory

Circle the letter of the best answer for each question.

10. What is one way that animals save energy?

a. flying at night

b. building large homes

c. avoiding competition

d. hunting during the day

11. Which is something that animals do NOT use their territories for?

a. mating

b. migrating

c. raising their young

d. finding food

Circle the letter of the best answer for each question.

12. How do some birds mark their territory?

a. singing

b. building a nest

c. flapping their wings

d. dropping their feathers

Defensive Action

Read the words in the box. Read the sentences. Fill in each blank with the word or phrase that best completes the sentence.

predators	acid
defend	distraction

13. Animals ______________________ territories, food, mates, and offspring.

14. Animals use defensive behaviors to protect themselves from ______________________.

15. Some birds use ______________________ to defend their young.

16. Bees, ants, and wasps inject a powerful ______________________ into their attackers.

Courtship and Parenting

Read the words in the box. Read the sentences. Fill in the blanks with the word or phrase that best completes the sentence.

nests	parents	courtship
hunt	food	

17. Animals use ______________________ behaviors to help them find mates.

18. Some birds and fish build ______________________ to attract mates.

19. Many young animals depend on their ______________________ for survival.

20. Some adult birds bring ______________________ to their young.

21. Adult killer whales teach their young how to ______________________.

SEASONAL BEHAVIOR

Migration

Read the words in the box. Read the sentences. Fill in each blank with the word or phrase that best completes the sentence.

landmarks	migrate	food or water
monarch butterflies	Northern Hemisphere	

22. Birds in the ______________________ fly south for the winter.

23. Central Mexico is an area where ______________________ migrate to wait for the spring.

24. To ______________________ is to travel from one place to another.

25. Animals may migrate to find ______________________.

26. Many animals use ______________________ to find their way along migration paths.

Slowing Down

Read the description. Then, draw a line from the dot next to each description to the matching word.

27. hibernate to deal with winter food and water shortages ●

28. burrow in the mud to hide from the cold ●

29. store food to prepare for the winter ●

30. estivate to deal with summer food and water shortages ●

31. slow down but do not enter deep hibernation ●

a. bears

b. mice, squirrels, and skunks

c. frogs

d. desert squirrels and desert mice

e. squirrels

A Biological Clock

Read the words in the box. Read the sentences. Fill in each blank with the word or phrase that best completes the sentence.

temperature	time	seasonal cycles
biological clock	circadian rhythms	

32. Animals need to keep track of ______________________ so they know when to sleep and when to migrate.

33. The internal control of an animal's natural cycles is called a(n) ______________________.

34. Animals use the length of the day and the ______________________ to set their clocks.

35. Some animals have biological clocks that keep track of daily cycles that are called ______________________.

36. Hibernation, reproduction, and migration are three behaviors that can be controlled by ______________________.

Name ______________________ Class ______________ Date ____________

Skills Worksheet

Directed Reading B

Section: Social Relationships

Circle the letter of the best answer for each question.

1. What is it called when animals interact with each other?

a. defensive actions

b. social behavior

c. circadian rhythms

d. migration

2. Animals depend on this for their social interactions.

a. competition

b. courtship

c. food and water

d. communication

COMMUNICATION

3. Humans use this to communicate.

a. language

b. biological clocks

c. hibernation

d. distraction

4. To communicate, one of these must travel from one animal to another animal.

a. estivation

b. signal

c. innate behavior

d. seasonal behavior

Circle the letter of the best answer for each question.

5. Which is NOT a reason that animals use communication?

a. to defend their territory

b. to learn an innate behavior

c. to find food

d. to warn others of danger

6. Which is NOT a reason that animals use communication?

a. to find mates

b. to identify family members

c. to frighten predators

d. to set their internal clocks

WAYS TO COMMUNICATE

Sound

Read the description. Then, draw a line from the dot next to each description to the matching word.

7. sing songs to tell other members of their species where they are ●

8. make whistles and clicking noises ●

9. howl to defend their territory ●

10. can reach many animals over a large area ●

a. humpback whales

b. dolphins

c. sound

d. wolves

Touch

Circle the letter of the best answer for each question.

11. What kind of communication are chimpanzees using when they groom each other?

a. sound

b. touch

c. chemical

d. sight

Chemicals

<u>Circle the letter</u> of the best answer for each question.

12. What are the chemicals that animals use to communicate called?

a. estivation

b. migration

c. pheromones

d. hibernation

13. What do many animals use pheromones for?

a. to attract a mate

b. to groom

c. to comfort one another

d. to digest food

Sight

Read the words in the box. Read the sentences. <u>Fill in each blank</u> with the word or phrase that best completes the sentence.

food	attract
body language	feathers

14. When humans smile, they are using ______________________ to send a visual message.

15. Bees spread the news about ______________________ by using body language.

16. An animal may ruffle its ______________________ to look bigger.

17. Fireflies blink signals to ______________________ mates.

LIVING TOGETHER

The Benefits of Living in a Group

Read the words in the box. Read the sentences. Fill in each blank with the word or phrase that best completes the sentence.

defend	predator
food	larger prey

18. Large groups of animals can spot a ______________________ quickly.

19. Groups can work together to ______________________ themselves.

20. Living together helps animals find ______________________.

21. Animals that hunt in groups can kill ______________________.

The Downside of Living in Groups

move around	food and mates
predators	look out

22. Animals living in a group must compete for ______________________.

23. When an area doesn't have enough food, animals must ______________________ to search for food.

24. Animals that live in groups often attract ______________________.

25. Animals in groups must ______________________ for predators.

Name ________________________ Class ______________ Date ______________

Assessment

Chapter Test C

Animals and Behavior

MULTIPLE CHOICE

Circle the letter of the best answer for each question.

1. What do some animals use to find their way when they migrate?

a. landmarks
b. body language
c. courtship
d. circadian rhythms

2. What kind of communication is a dolphin using when it whistles or clicks?

a. chemicals
b. sound
c. touch
d. sight

3. What behavior do animals use to protect their territories, food, mates, and offspring?

a. migration
b. courtship behavior
c. defensive behavior
d. reproduction

4. What kind of communication is body language?

a. touch
b. sound
c. sight
d. chemical

5. What is it called when an adult animal takes care of its baby?

a. estivation
b. hibernation
c. courtship
d. parenting

6. What kind of communication are chimpanzees using when they groom each other?

a. sight
b. touch
c. courtship
d. chemical

Circle the letter of the best answer for each question.

7. What are an animal's daily cycles called?

a. circadian rhythms

b. internal changes

c. communication

d. seasonal cycles

8. Which of the following is NOT something all animals do?

a. reproduce

b. have specialized parts

c. eat

d. hibernate

9. How are innate behaviors inherited?

a. through learned behavior

b. through genes

c. through seasonal cycles

d. through hibernation

10. What is an area occupied by an animal or group of animals called?

a. a territory

b. a pheromone

c. a distraction

d. a competition

11. What are animals that are eaten by other animals called?

a. pheromones

b. consumers

c. predators

d. prey

MATCHING

Read the description. Then, draw a line from the dot next to each description to the matching word.

12. a group of similar cells

13. a group of tissues that carry out a special function of the body

14. an animal with a backbone

15. a chemical used for communication

a. organ

b. invertebrate

c. tissue

d. pheromone

---

16. an organism at an early stage of development

17. an organism that eats other organisms

18. an organism part that breaks off and grows into a new organism

19. an organism made up of many cells

a. embryo

b. consumer

c. multicellular

d. budding

FILL-IN-THE-BLANK

Read the words in the box. Read the sentences. Fill in each blank with the word or phrase that best completes the sentence.

courtship	social
migrating	seasonal cycles

20. When animals travel from one place to another, they are ______________________.

21. Hibernation and migration are behaviors that are controlled by ______________________.

22. An animal uses ______________________ behavior to find a mate.

23. When animals interact with each other, it is called ______________________ behavior.

Name ______________________ Class ______________ Date ____________

Skills Worksheet

Directed Reading B

Section: Simple Invertebrates

Circle the letter of the best answer for each question.

1. What are animals without backbones called?

a. invertebrates

b. species

c. mammals

d. backless

INVERTEBRATE CHARACTERISTICS

2. What makes invertebrates alike?

a. They all have mouths.

b. They all have heads.

c. They are all worms.

d. They don't have backbones.

Draw a line from each term to the matching number on the picture.

asymmetry   bilateral symmetry   radial symmetry

3.

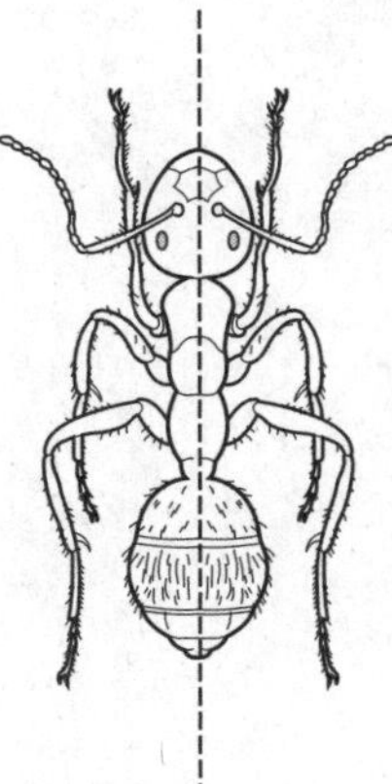

4.

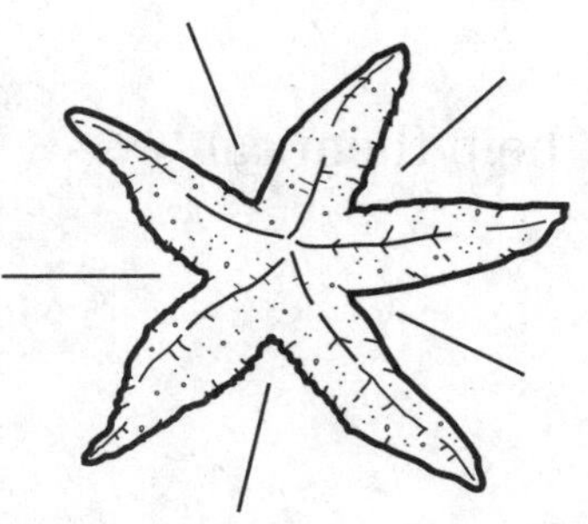

5.

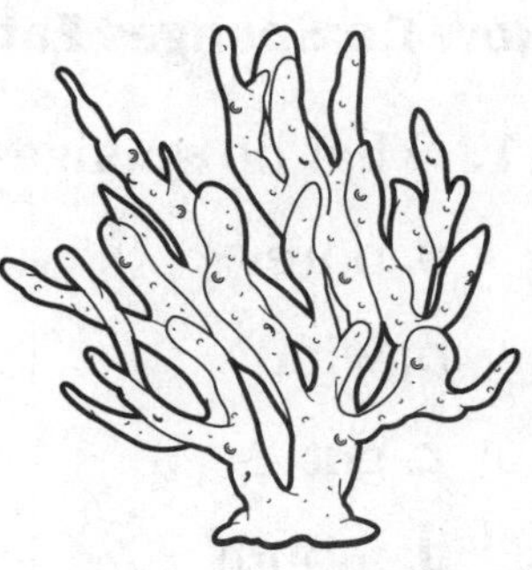

Nerves

Circle the letter of the best answer for the question.

6. What do nerves do?

a. create a backbone

b. digest food

c. carry messages

d. arrange cords

Read the description. Then, draw a line from the dot next to each description to the matching word.

7. where animals digest food	●	**a.** ganglion
8. body cavity that surrounds the gut	●	**b.** gut
9. mass of nerve cells	●	**c.** coelem

SPONGES

Circle the letter of the best answer for each question.

10. Why are sponges not called plants?

a. Sponges move too much.

b. Sponges are too big.

c. Sponges can't make food.

d. Sponges have bright colors.

How Do Sponges Eat?

11. What do sponges use to help them eat?

a. pores

b. wind

c. gut

d. mouth

Circle the letter of the best answer for each question.

12. What do collar cells help a sponge to do?

a. breathe

b. eat

c. move

d. sleep

Body Part Abilities

13. What can a sponge do if a body part breaks off?

a. eat it

b. move away

c. grow it back

d. die

14. If a sponge is broken into pieces, what will happen?

a. The sponge will eat.

b. The sponge will reproduce.

c. The sponge will build a shell.

d. The sponge will filter water.

Kinds of Sponges

15. What is a spicule?

a. shell

b. sponge's mouth

c. kind of sponge

d. sponge's skeleton

CNIDARIANS

Circle the letter of the best answer for each question.

16. What do all cnidarians have?

a. coral

b. polyps

c. stinging cells

d. medusas

17. How are some cnidarians like sponges?

a. Cnidarians can move quickly.

b. Cnidarians have shells.

c. Cnidarians can re-form.

d. Cnidarians have a gut.

Two Body Forms

18. What cnidarian body form usually swims free?

a. medusa

b. polyp

c. sponge

d. mollusk

19. Which cnidarian body form usually stays attached to a surface?

a. medusa

b. polyp

c. sponge

d. mollusk

Stinging Cells

Circle the letter of the best answer for the question.

20. What do cnidarians use their stinging cells for?

a. clean themselves

b. fix themselves

c. digest food

d. protect themselves

Kinds of Cnidarians

Read the description. Then, draw a line from the dot next to each description to the matching word.

21. use tentacles to catch fish ●	**a.** hydrozoans
22. spend their entire lives as polyps ●	**b.** jellyfish
23. build big reefs ●	**c.** corals

FLATWORMS

Circle the letter of the best answer for each question.

24. What distinguishes flatworms from other kinds of worms?

a. They are the roundest worms.

b. They are the simplest worms.

c. They are parasites.

d. They are planarians.

25. What body plan do all flatworms have?

a. bilateral symmetry

b. polyps

c. asymmetry

d. medusa

Circle the letter of the best answer for each question.

26. What do flatworms use sensory lobes to do?

a. move

b. find food

c. focus

d. protect themselves

Planarians

27. What do a planarian's head, eyespots, and lobes indicate?

a. It is a predator.

b. It has a well-developed nervous system.

c. It can eat with its mouth.

d. It does not have a backbone.

Flukes

28. Flukes feed on living organisms. What is this kind of animal called?

a. planarian

b. predator

c. parasite

d. polyp

Tapeworms

Read the description. Then, draw a line from the dot next to each description to the matching word.

29. parasites with special suckers and hooks ●

30. predators with sensory lobes ●

31. parasites that absorb food without a gut ●

a. planarians

b. flukes

c. tapeworms

ROUNDWORMS

Circle the letter of the best answer for each question.

32. Which of these items is shaped like a roundworm's body?

a. a banana

b. a spoon

c. a piece of spaghetti

d. a ruler

33. How many roundworms can live in a single apple?

a. 100

b. 1,000

c. 100,000

d. 1,000,000

Name ______________________ Class ______________ Date ____________

Skills Worksheet

Directed Reading B

Section: Mollusks and Annelid Worms

Circle the letter of the best answer for each question.

1. Which of these is sometimes seen on the sidewalk after it rains?

a. flatworms

b. roundworms

c. earthworms

d. tapeworms

MOLLUSKS

Read the description. Then, draw a line from the dot next to each description to the matching word.

2. squids and octopuses	●	**a.** gastropods
3. shellfish with two shells	●	**b.** cephalopods
4. slugs and snails	●	**c.** bivalves

How Do Mollusks Eat?

5. use tentacles to grab food	●	**a.** snails and slugs
6. use gills to filter food	●	**b.** octopuses and squids
7. use a radula to scrape food	●	**c.** clams and oysters

Name ______________________ Class ______________ Date ____________

Ganglia and Brains

Circle the letter of the best answer for each question.

8. What do all mollusks have?

a. radula

b. complex ganglia

c. gills

d. tentacles

9. What are considered to be the smartest invertebrates?

a. cephalopods

b. gastropods

c. bivalves

d. flatworms

Pumping Blood

Read the description. Then, draw a line from the dot next to each description to the matching word.

10. pumps blood into sinuses	●	**a.** closed circulatory system
11. pumps blood through a closed loop	●	**b.** open circulatory system

Mollusk Bodies

Read the words in the box. Read the sentences. Fill in each blank with the word or phrase that best completes the sentence.

mantle	shell	foot	visceral mass

12. A mollusk moves using a powerful ______________________.

13. Gills and guts are a part of a ______________________.

14. A layer of tissue called a ______________________ protects mollusks that don't have shells.

15. A hard outer layer called a ______________________ protects some mollusks from predators.

ANNELID WORMS

Circle the letter of the best answer for each question.

16. What is another name for annelid worms?

a. roundworms
b. segmented worms
c. closed worms
d. flatworms

Earthworms

17. How many segments do earthworms have?

a. 3
b. 1,000
c. 100 to 175
d. 500 to 700

Circle the letter of the best answer for each question.

18. What do earthworms use to move?

a. legs

b. bristles

c. a foot

d. a shell

Marine Worms

19. What are marine worms covered with?

a. bristles

b. legs

c. mollusks

d. nerves

Leeches

20. What are leeches NOT known as?

a. cnidarians

b. parasites

c. predators

d. scavengers

21. What do doctors sometimes use leeches to do?

a. perform surgery

b. close wounds

c. heal the flu

d. help prevent swelling

Name ______________________ Class ______________ Date ____________

Skills Worksheet

Directed Reading B

Section: Arthropods

Circle the letter of the best answer for each question.

1. Which is the largest group of animals?

a. sponges

b. humans

c. arthropods

d. mollusks

CHARACTERISTICS OF ARTHROPODS

Segmented and Specialized

2. How many main body parts do most arthropods have?

a. sixteen

b. three

c. one

d. four

Jointed Limbs

3. What do jointed limbs help arthropods do?

a. move

b. hunt

c. fight

d. sleep

An External Skeleton

4. Where is an exoskeleton located?

a. in the head

b. inside the body

c. around the bones

d. outside the body

Circle the letter of the best answer for each question.

5. What is an exoskeleton made of?

a. organs

b. chitin

c. jointed limbs

d. nerves

6. What is an exoskeleton like?

a. suit of clothes

b. closed system

c. suit of armor

d. gills

Sensing Surroundings

Read the description. Then, draw a line from the dot next to each description to the matching word.

7. eye composed of many light detectors ●

8. eye that can see light but cannot see images ●

9. organ that can sense vibration ●

10. organ that receives information ●

a. bristle

b. simple eye

c. brain

d. compound eye

KINDS OF ARTHROPODS

Circle the letter of the best answer for each question.

11. How are arthropods grouped together?

a. by the way they see

b. by the kinds of body parts they have

c. by number of legs

d. by their shells

Read the words in the box. Read the sentences. Fill in each blank with the word or phrase that best completes the sentence.

mandible	antenna	chelicerae
cephalothorax	insect	gills

12. A feeler that senses touch, taste, or smell is known as

a(n) ______________________.

Centipedes and Millipedes

13. A mouthpart that can pierce and suck food is called

a(n) ______________________.

Crustaceans

14. Crustaceans use ______________________ to breathe.

Arachnids

15. The head and thorax of a spider is called the

______________________.

16. A clawlike mouthpart of a spider is called a(n)

______________________.

Insects

17. An animal with six legs and antennae is called a(n)

______________________.

THE WORLD OF INSECTS

Insect Bodies

Circle the letter of the best answer for each question.

18. How many pairs of antennae do insects have?

a. one

b. two

c. none

d. four

19. What do insects use to see?

a. sensory lobes

b. bristles

c. simple eyes

d. compound eyes

Complete Metamorphosis

Read the description. Then, draw a line from the dot next to each description to the matching stage of metamorphosis.

20. The caterpillar becomes a pupa.

21. A larva hatches from an egg.

22. Adult body parts replace the larval body parts.

23. An adult lays eggs.

24. The adult butterfly pumps blood into its wings.

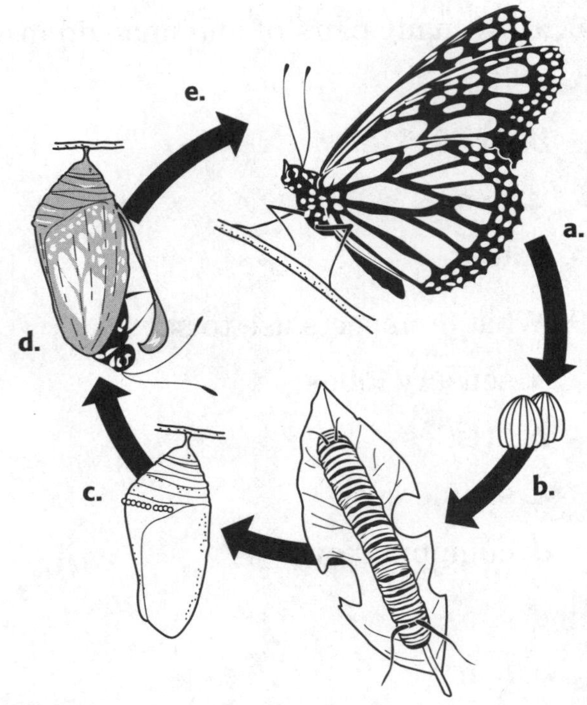

Incomplete Metamorphosis

Circle the letter of the best answer for the question.

25. How is incomplete metamorphosis different from complete metamorphosis?

a. It is quicker.

b. It is less complicated.

c. It lasts longer.

d. It does not involve eggs.

Name ______________________ Class ______________ Date ____________

Skills Worksheet

Directed Reading B

Section: Echinoderms

Circle the letter of the best answer for each question.

1. Where do all echinoderms live?

a. lakes and rivers

b. everywhere

c. the ocean

d. land

SPINY SKINNED

2. What is an echinoderm's internal skeleton called?

a. spicules

b. endoskeleton

c. exoskeleton

d. bones

BILATERAL OR RADIAL?

3. Adult echinoderms have radial symmetry. What kind do their larvae have?

a. radial symmetry

b. bilateral symmetry

c. asymmetry

d. compound symmetry

THE NERVOUS SYSTEM

4. Which word describes an echinoderm's nervous system?

a. bilateral

b. unique

c. complex

d. simple

Read the description. Then, draw a line from the dot next to each description to the matching word.

5. senses light

6. controls arm movement

7. circle of nerve fibers around the mouth

a. radial nerve

b. nerve ring

c. simple eye

WATER VASCULAR SYSTEM

Circle the letter of the best answer for each question.

8. What does the water vascular system help echinoderms to do?

a. move, breathe, and eat

b. sleep

c. reproduce

d. regenerate

KINDS OF ECHINODERMS

Read the description. Then, draw a line from the dot next to each description to the matching word.

9. round, with a shell-like endoskeleton

10. have a wormlike shape

11. have long, slim arms

12. have many feathery arms

a. brittle stars and basket stars

b. sea urchins and sand dollars

c. sea lilies and feather stars

d. sea cucumbers

Name ______________________ Class ______________ Date ____________

Assessment

Chapter Test C

Simple Invertebrates

Circle the letter of the best answer for each question.

1. What does the word *invertebrate* mean?

a. an animal that has no backbone

b. an animal that is a parasite

c. an animal that has no head

d. an animal that has no skeleton

2. What do parasites feed on?

a. material in soil

b. dead animals

c. living animals

d. each other

3. Which of these is a bundle of nerve cells?

a. gut

b. tube foot

c. ganglion

d. eye

4. What do jellyfish and coral both have?

a. tube feet

b. skeletons

c. stinging cells

d. wings

5. What do mollusks use to move?

a. bristles

b. mantle

c. a foot

d. gills

6. What protects mollusks that don't have shells?

a. mantle

b. sinuses

c. gills

d. visceral mass

Circle the letter of the best answer for each question.

7. What do bristles help an earthworm to do?

a. feed
b. sleep
c. move
d. stay clean

8. What helps a sea star to move, eat, and breathe?

a. simple nervous system
b. water vascular system
c. endoskeleton
d. closed circulatory system

9. What kind of skeleton is like a suit of armor?

a. shell
b. endoskeleton
c. spiny skeleton
d. exoskeleton

10. What can a simple eye see?

a. images
b. pressure
c. chemicals
d. light

11. What is a mandible?

a. claw
b. foot
c. mouthpart
d. nerve cell

12. Which kind of metamorphosis is less complicated?

a. reproduction
b. incomplete metamorphosis
c. regeneration
d. complete metamorphosis

MATCHING

Read the description. Then, <u>draw a line</u> from the dot next to each description to the matching word.

13. animals that have spiny skeletons ●

14. animals that have jointed limbs and specialized parts ●

15. animals that have many segments ●

a. annelid worms

b. arthropods

c. echinoderms

---

16. animal that has three main body parts, six legs, and one pair of antennae ●

17. animal that has a cephalothorax and an abdomen ●

18. animal that has stinging cells ●

19. animal that is very simple ●

a. arachnid

b. cnidarian

c. sponge

d. insect

FILL-IN-THE-BLANK

Read the words in the box Read the sentences. Fill in each blank with the word or phrase that best completes the sentence.

bilateral symmetry	radial symmetry
asymmetrical	regeneration

20. The process of regrowing a missing part is called

______________________________.

21. The kind of symmetry that goes around a center is

called ______________________________.

22. The kind of symmetry where two sides mirror each other is

called ______________________________.

23. An animal that has no symmetry is ______________________________.

Name ______________________ Class ______________ Date ______________

Skills Worksheet

Directed Reading B

Section: Fishes: The First Vertebrates

Circle the letter of the best answer for each question.

1. What are animals that have a backbone called?

a. endotherms
b. ectotherms
c. chordates
d. vertebrates

CHORDATES

2. What is the largest group of chordates?

a. lancelets
b. fishes
c. vertebrates
d. tunicates

3. Which of the following is NOT a body part that every chordate has?

a. tail
b. backbone
c. notochord
d. hollow nerve cord

VERTEBRATE CHARACTERISTICS

4. What are the bones that form the backbone called?

a. vertebrae
b. skull
c. cartilage
d. notochord

5. What is the tough, flexible material in our ears and nose?

a. vertebrae
b. embryo
c. cartilage
d. notochord

ARE VERTEBRATES WARM OR COLD?

Staying Warm

Circle the letter of the best answer for each question.

6. What are animals that have a stable body temperature called?

a. vertebrates

b. ectotherms

c. coldblooded

d. endotherms

Cold Blood?

7. What is the name for animals that depend on their surroundings to stay warm?

a. vertebrates

b. ectotherms

c. warmblooded

d. endotherms

FISH CHARACTERISTICS

Read the description. Then, draw a line from the dot next to each description to the matching word.

8. what fish use to steer, stop, and balance ●

9. bony structures that protect some fishes' bodies ●

10. rows of sense organs along each side of a fish ●

11. the organs fish use to breathe ●

a. scales

b. fins

c. gills

d. lateral lines

Making More Fish

Circle the letter of the best answer for each question.

12. How do most fish reproduce?

a. internal fertilization

b. asexual reproduction

c. external fertilization

d. unfertilized eggs

KINDS OF FISHES

13. How many different classes of fishes exist today?

a. two

b. three

c. four

d. five

Jawless Fishes

14. Which of the following is NOT a trait of jawless fish?

a. They are eel-like.

b. They have a skull, brain, and eyes.

c. Their skeleton is made of cartilage.

d. They use jaws to eat.

Cartilaginous Fishes

15. Which is NOT a cartilaginous fish?

a. goldfish

b. skate

c. shark

d. ray

16. Which is NOT a trait of cartilaginous fishes?

a. They are strong swimmers.

b. They have a bony skeleton.

c. They are expert predators.

d. They have a lateral line system.

Bony Fishes

Circle the letter of the best answer for each question.

17. Which is NOT a bony fish?

a. goldfish

b. tuna

c. catfish

d. shark

18. Which is NOT a trait of bony fishes?

a. They have a swim bladder.

b. They have scales.

c. They are eel-like.

d. They have a bony skeleton.

19. Which is a group of bony fishes?

a. ray-finned fishes

b. vultures of the sea

c. hagfish

d. stingrays

20. What is the organ that keeps bony fishes from sinking?

a. gall bladder

b. swim bladder

c. gill

d. oily liver

21. Which fishes may be related to the ancestors of amphibians?

a. ray-finned fishes

b. lobe-finned fishes

c. cartilaginous fishes

d. jawless fishes

Name ______________________________ Class ______________ Date ____________

Skills Worksheet

Directed Reading B

Section: Amphibians

MOVING TO LAND

Circle the letter of the best answer for each question.

1. Which is NOT a trait of amphibians?

a. They can live in water.

b. They have legs.

c. They get oxygen from the air.

d. They have fins.

CHARACTERISTICS OF AMPHIBIANS

Read the words in the box. Read the sentences. Fill in each blank with the word that best completes the sentence.

amphibian	tadpoles	lungs	metamorphosis

2. Amphibians can breathe by gulping air into their

______________________________.

3. "Double life" is the meaning of ______________________________.

4. After hatching, frog or toad embryos become

______________________________.

5. The change from an immature form to an adult form is called

______________________________.

KINDS OF AMPHIBIANS

Circle the letter of the best answer for each question.

6. How many groups of amphibians are there?

a. one

b. two

c. three

d. four

7. Which is NOT a group of amphibians?

a. caecilians

b. salamanders

c. frogs and toads

d. lizards

Caecilians

8. What type of animal do caecilians look like?

a. salamanders

b. tadpoles

c. earthworms or snakes

d. frogs

9. What feature do other amphibians have that caecilians do not have?

a. lungs

b. thin skin

c. moist skin

d. legs

Salamanders

Circle the letter of the best answer for each question.

10. Where do most salamanders live?

a. Asia

b. South America

c. Africa

d. North America

Frogs and Toads

11. What percentage of amphibians are either frogs or toads?

a. 30%

b. 70%

c. 50%

d. 90%

Singing Frogs

12. What is the thin-walled sac of skin that surrounds a frog's vocal chords called?

a. vocal sac

b. vibrating sac

c. acoustic sac

d. singing sac

AMPHIBIANS AS ECOLOGICAL INDICATORS

13. Why are amphibians good ecological indicators?

a. They can live in any environment.

b. They are sensitive to environmental change.

c. They can change their body temperature.

d. They can repel chemicals with their skin.

Name ______________________ Class ______________ Date ____________

Skills Worksheet

Directed Reading B

Section: Reptiles

LIVING ON LAND

Circle the letter of the best answer for each question.

1. How are reptiles different from amphibians?

a. Reptiles breathe through gills.

b. Reptiles can spend their whole lives on land.

c. Reptiles lay eggs.

d. Some reptiles are now extinct.

CHARACTERISTICS OF REPTILES

2. Which is NOT a characteristic of reptiles?

a. They have lungs.

b. They have thick skin.

c. They can control their body temperatures.

d. They have special eggs.

Thick Skin

3. Why is thick, dry skin important to reptiles?

a. It protects them from predators.

b. It helps them absorb oxygen.

c. It helps them lose water quickly.

d. It keeps them from losing water.

Body Temperature

4. When are reptiles most active?

a. When it is cold.

b. When it is warm.

c. When it is rainy.

d. When it is dry.

The Amazing Amniotic Egg

<u>Circle the letter</u> of the best answer for each question.

5. What part of a reptile's egg keeps the egg from drying out?

a. albumen
b. allantois
c. shell
d. amniotic sac

Parts of the Amniotic Egg

Read the description. Then, <u>draw a line</u> from the dot next to each description to the matching word.

6. gives the embryo a rich supply of food ●
7. stores the embryo's wastes ●
8. provides water and protein to the embryo ●
9. protects the egg from damage ●

a. shell
b. albumen
c. yolk
d. allantois

Reptile Reproduction

<u>Circle the letter</u> of the best answer for each question.

10. How do reptiles usually reproduce?

a. internal fertilization
b. external fertilization
c. metamorphosis
d. unfertilized eggs

KINDS OF REPTILES

11. How many groups of reptiles live today?

a. two
b. three
c. four
d. five

12. Which is NOT a group of reptiles?

a. turtles and tortoises
b. frogs
c. crocodiles and alligators
d. tuataras

Turtles and Tortoises

Circle the letter of the best answer for each question.

13. What makes turtles and tortoises different than other reptiles?

a. their ability to lay eggs

b. their ability to control their body temperatures

c. their thick skin

d. their shells

Crocodiles and Alligators

14. How are crocodiles different from alligators?

a. Crocodiles have eyes on top of their heads.

b. Crocodiles eat meat.

c. Crocodiles have pointed snouts.

d. Crocodiles spend most of their time in the water.

Snakes and Lizards

15. What trait do snakes NOT have?

a. Snakes can break off their tails to escape predators.

b. Some snakes have fangs for injecting venom.

c. Snakes are carnivores.

d. Snakes open their mouths very wide when they eat.

Tuataras

16. What other reptile does a tuatara look like?

a. lizard

b. crocodile

c. snake

d. turtle

17. When are tuataras most active?

a. during the day

b. during the winter

c. during the night

d. during rainy weather

Name ______________________ Class ______________ Date ____________

Assessment

Chapter Test C

Fishes, Amphibians, and Reptiles

MULTIPLE CHOICE

Circle the letter of the best answer for each question.

1. Which is NOT a common body part of a chordate?

a. pharyngeal pouch

b. lancelet

c. notochord

d. hollow nerve cord

2. Which of the following is a jawless fish?

a. lamprey

b. goldfish

c. skate

d. shark

3. Which is NOT a trait of cartilaginous fishes?

a. They are strong swimmers.

b. They have a bony skeleton.

c. They are expert predators.

d. They have oily livers.

4. Which is NOT a trait of bony fishes?

a. They have a swim bladder.

b. They can rest without swimming.

c. They are eel-like.

d. They have a bony skeleton.

MULTIPLE CHOICE

Circle the letter of the best answer for each question.

5. Which is NOT a group of amphibians?

a. caecilians

b. salamanders

c. frogs and toads

d. lizards

6. What type of animal do caecilians look like?

a. salamanders

b. tadpoles

c. earthworms

d. frogs

7. What is the thin-walled sac of skin that surrounds a frog's vocal cords called?

a. vocal sac

b. vibrating sac

c. swim bladder

d. scales

8. How do reptiles usually reproduce?

a. internal fertilization

b. external fertilization

c. metamorphosis

d. unfertilized eggs

MATCHING

Read the description. Then, draw a line from the dot next to each description to the matching word.

9. the tough material that the flexible parts of our ears and nose are made of ●

10. an animal that has a stable body temperature ●

11. an animal that has a backbone ●

12. an animal that depends on its environment for heat ●

a. vertebrate

b. cartilage

c. endotherm

d. ectotherm

---

13. a row of tiny sense organs that detects water vibrations ●

14. a gas-filled sac that helps bony fishes float ●

15. the organ that fish use to breathe ●

a. lateral line

b. gill

c. swim bladder

FILL-IN-THE-BLANK

Read the words in the box. Read the sentences. Fill in each blank with the word or phrase that best completes the sentence.

amphibians	amniotic eggs	lung
tadpoles	metamorphosis	

16. Reptiles, birds, and mammals have ______________________ that protect the embryo.

17. Animals that live both on water and on land are called ______________________.

18. When an immature form of an animal changes to an adult form, it has gone through ______________________.

19. The saclike organ that allows amphibians to breathe is the ______________________.

20. Immature frogs or toads that must live in the water are ______________________.

Name ______________________ Class ______________ Date ____________

Skills Worksheet

Directed Reading B

Section: Characteristics of Birds

Circle the letter of the best answer for each question.

1. What do birds and reptiles have in common?

a. horny beaks

b. feathers and wings

c. thick scales on legs

d. endothermic bodies

FEATHERS

2. How do feathers help birds?

a. Feathers help birds keep warm.

b. Feathers help birds perch on branches.

c. Feathers help birds build nests.

d. Feathers help birds find food.

Preening and Molting

Read the words in the box. Read the sentences. Fill in each blank with the word or phrase that best completes the sentence.

preening	molting

3. Birds that groom their feathers are ______________________.

4. Birds that lose feathers and grow new ones are

______________________.

Two Kinds of Feathers

Read the words in the box. Read the sentences. Fill in each blank with the word or phrase that best completes the sentence.

down feathers	contour feathers

5. Feathers that cover a bird's body and wings are called

______________________________.

6. Feathers close to a bird's body that keep it warm are called

______________________________.

HIGH-ENERGY ANIMALS

Circle the letter of the best answer for each question.

7. Why do birds need a lot of energy?

a. to eat

b. to fly

c. to build nests

d. to keep cool

FAST DIGESTION

Read the description. Then draw a line from the dot next to each description to the matching word.

8. Swallowed food is stored here. ●

9. Food is ground with small stones here. ●

10. Food is digested here. ●

a. gizzard

b. crop

c. intestine

FLYING

Read the description. Then, draw a line from the dot next to each description to the matching characteristic of the bird.

11. keel

12. powerful flight muscles

13. light skeleton

14. wings

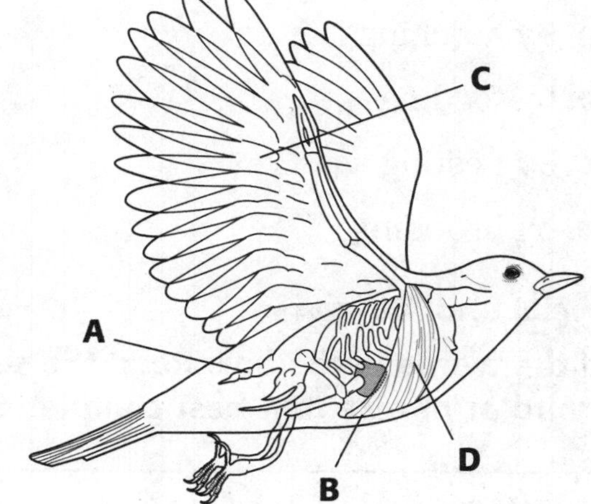

GETTING OFF THE GROUND

Circle the letter of the best answer for each question.

15. What is the upward force on a flying bird's wings called?

a. gravity

b. wind

c. lift

d. pressure

RAISING BABY BIRDS

16. How do birds reproduce?

a. by internal fertilization

b. by asexual means

c. by nesting

d. by brooding

Nests

Circle the letter of the best answer for each question.

17. How do birds keep their eggs warm?

a. by hatching

b. by feeding

c. by nesting

d. by brooding

Precocial and Altricial

Read the words in the box. Read the sentences. Fill in each blank with the word or phrase that best completes the sentence.

precocial	altricial

18. Birds that are active soon after birth are called

______________________.

19. Young birds that are weak and must be fed by parents are called

______________________.

Name ______________________ Class ______________ Date ____________

Skills Worksheet

Directed Reading B

Section: Kinds of Birds

FLIGHTLESS BIRDS

Circle the letter of the best answer for each question.

1. How do flightless birds move around?

a. dive and run

b. swim and dive

c. swim and run

d. hop and dive

2. Which of the following is a flightless bird?

a. crow

b. kiwi

c. robin

d. owl

WATER BIRDS

3. What is a special adaptation of water birds?

a. oily feathers

b. long necks

c. bright colors

d. webbed feet

4. What of the following is a water bird?

a. chickadee

b. ostrich

c. blue-footed booby

d. parrot

PERCHING BIRDS

<u>Circle the letter</u> of the best answer for each question.

5. What is a special adaptation of perching birds?

a. feet that close around branches

b. nest-building skills

c. ability to soar

d. short beaks

6. Which of the following is a perching bird?

a. loon

b. penguin

c. wood duck

d. sparrow

BIRDS OF PREY

7. How do birds of prey use sharp beaks and claws?

a. to grasp branches

b. to build strong nests

c. to catch and eat food

d. to dive into the water

8. Which of the following is a bird of prey?

a. osprey

b. robin

c. crane

d. ostrich

Name ______________________ Class ______________ Date ____________

Skills Worksheet

Directed Reading B

Section: Characteristics of Mammals

THE FIRST MAMMALS

Circle the letter of the best answer for each question.

1. About what size were the first mammals?

a. the size of mice
b. the size of dogs
c. the size of horses
d. the size of elephants

2. What trait allowed early mammals to hunt at night?

a. They had claws.
b. They could swim.
c. They were endotherms.
d. They were like reptiles.

COMMON CHARACTERISTICS

3. How are dolphins, monkeys, and elephants like people?

a. They are not predators.
b. They can swim.
c. They have hair and special teeth.
d. They can live in any climate.

Making Milk

Read the words in the box. Read the sentences. Fill in each blank with the word or phrase that best completes the sentence.

mammary	protein

4. In a female mammal, the gland that makes milk is the

______________________ gland.

5. All milk is made of water, sugars, fats, and

______________________.

Breathing Air

Circle the letter of the best answer for each question.

6. What large muscle helps bring air into the lungs?

a. mammary gland

b. rib cage

c. diaphragm

d. air sac

Endothermic

7. What is an endotherm?

a. An animal with a constant body temperature.

b. An animal with a high body temperature.

c. An animal with a low body temperature.

d. An animal with no body temperature.

8. Which of the following animals are endotherms?

a. reptiles

b. fish

c. amphibians

d. birds

Hair

Read the words in the box. Read the sentences. Fill in each blank with the word or phrase that best completes the sentence.

fur	blubber

9. Mammals such as whales have a thick layer of fat called

______________________ to keep them warm.

10. Mammals living in cold climates have thick coats of hair called

______________________ to keep them warm.

Specialized Teeth

Read the words in the box. Read the sentences. Fill in each blank with the word or phrase that best completes the sentence.

incisors	canines	molars

11. Flat, grinding teeth are called ______________________.

12. Cutting teeth are called ______________________.

13. Teeth for stabbing are called ______________________.

Sexual Reproduction

Circle the letter of the best answer for each question.

14. Where is the egg fertilized by the sperm in mammals?

a. inside the female's body

b. outside the female's body

c. inside the male's body

d. outside the male's body

15. How long does a young mammal stay with a parent?

a. until shortly after birth

b. for one month

c. for one year

d. until it is grown

Large Brains

16. Which of the following is NOT true of a mammal's brain?

a. It is larger than the brains of most other animals that are the same size.

b. It forces mammals to sleep through the night.

c. It allows mammals to respond quickly to events.

d. It allows mammals to use all five senses.

Name ______________________ Class ______________ Date ____________

Skills Worksheet

Directed Reading B

Section: Placental Mammals

Read the description. Then draw a line from the dot next to each description to the matching word.

1. An embryo grows in this organ.

2. This describes a mammal whose embryos develop inside the mother's body.

3. This organ attaches the embryo to the uterus.

4. This names the period the embryo develops inside its mother.

a. gestation period

b. uterus

c. placenta

d. placental mammal

ANTEATERS, ARMADILLOS, AND SLOTHS

Circle the letter of the best answer for each question.

5. What characteristic sets anteaters, armadillos, and sloths apart from other mammals?

a. They have no teeth.

b. They have an armor-like shell.

c. They have unique backbones.

d. They have unusual tails.

INSECTIVORES

6. What characteristics are found in all insectivores?

a. small brains and simple teeth

b. large brains and long noses

c. sharp teeth and furry bodies

d. good eyesight and no teeth

RODENTS

Circle the letter of the best answer for each question.

7. How do rodents use their strong, sharp teeth?

a. to catch prey

b. to chew and gnaw

c. to protect them from enemies

d. to attract mates

RABBITS, HARES, AND PIKAS

8. How are rabbits, hares, and pikas different from rodents?

a. Rabbits, hares, and pikas have more fur.

b. Rabbits, hares, and pikas have longer legs and ears.

c. Rabbits, hares, and pikas have two sets of incisors and shorter tails.

d. Rabbits, hares, and pikas have longer tails and shorter ears.

FLYING MAMMALS

9. Which of the following is the only flying mammal?

a. flying squirrel

b. bat

c. bird

d. pika

10. How are bats able to find food?

a. with good night vision

b. with a good sense of smell

c. with sharp teeth and claws

d. with echolocation

CARNIVORES

Read the description. Then draw a line from the dot next to each description to the matching word.

11. mammals with large canine teeth and special molars for slicing meat

12. meat-eating mammals that also eat plants

13. fish-eating ocean mammals

a. pinnipeds

b. carnivores

c. omnivores

TRUNK-NOSED MAMMALS

Circle the letter of the best answer for each question.

14. How do elephants use their trunks?

a. to fight off predators

b. to smell their food

c. to protect their young

d. to put food in their mouths

HOOFED MAMMALS

15. What is a hoof?

a. a claw

b. a thick, hard pad that covers a mammal's toe

c. a finger

d. a toe

16. What are two characteristics of hoofed mammals?

a. short fur and small, pointed teeth

b. long legs and long necks

c. large, flat molars and ability to run fast

d. long tails and slow movers

Circle the letter of the best answer for each question.

17. Which of the following hoofed mammals is odd-toed?

a. zebra

b. camel

c. deer

d. giraffe

18. Which of the following hoofed mammals is even-toed?

a. tapir

b. horse

c. rhinoceros

d. cattle

CETACEANS

19. How are cetaceans different from fish?

a. Cetaceans have lungs and nurse their young.

b. Cetaceans eat small sea life.

c. Cetaceans are covered with tiny scales.

d. Cetaceans breathe through gills and have fins.

MANATEES AND DUGONGS

20. Where do manatees and dugongs live?

a. only in the water

b. only on land

c. mostly in water; sometimes on land

d. mostly on land; sometimes in water

PRIMATES

Circle the letter of the best answer for each question.

21. Which of the following mammals is a primate?

a. spinner dolphin

b. orangutan

c. porcupine

d. sloth

Read the description. Then draw a line from the dot next to each description to the matching word.

20. allows focus on a single point	●	**a.** opposable thumbs
21. allows holding of objects	●	**b.** forward-facing eyes
22. allows swinging in trees	●	**c.** flexible shoulder joints

Name ______________________________ Class ______________ Date ____________

Skills Worksheet

Directed Reading B

Section: Monotremes and Marsupials

MONOTREMES

Circle the letter of the best answer for each question.

1. How does a monotreme differ from other mammals?

a. A monotreme lays eggs.

b. A monotreme keeps its body temperature constant.

c. A monotreme has spikes.

d. A monotreme feeds its young milk.

Echidnas

2. What features help the echnida find insects?

a. compact, thick body

b. very good eyesight

c. large claws and long snouts

d. long tail and strong shoulder muscles

The Platypus

Read the words in the box. Read the sentences. Fill in each blank with the word or phrase that best completes the sentence.

flat tail	rubbery bill

3. The platypus uses its ______________________________ to search for food.

4. To move through water, the platypus uses its webbed feet and ______________________________.

MARSUPIALS

Circle the letter of the best answer for each question.

5. Which of the following is a special feature of marsupials?

a. the fur

b. the pouch

c. the tail

d. the feet

6. What is the only living marsupial native to North America?

a. kangaroo

b. platypus

c. opossum

d. monotreme

The Pouch

Read the words in the box. Read the sentences. Fill in each blank with the word or phrase that best completes the sentence.

bumblebee	marsupial	joey

7. The young kangaroo is called a(n) ______________________.

8. The newborn kangaroo is about the size of a(n)

______________________.

9. The kangaroo is one example of a(n)

______________________.

Kinds of Marsupials

<u>Circle the letter</u> of the best answer for the question.

10. Where do most marsupials live?

a. South America

b. Australia

c. Africa

d. Asia

Endangered and Extinct Marsupials

Read the words in the box. Read the sentences. <u>Fill in each blank</u> with the word or phrase that best completes the sentence.

rabbits	foxes	Tasmanian tigers

11. Habitat destruction and hunting have hurt marsupials such as ______________________.

12. Non-native animals such as ______________________ compete with marsupials for food.

13. Non-native animals such as ______________________ prey on marsupials.

Name ______________________ Class ______________ Date ______________

Assessment

Chapter Test C

Birds and Mammals

MULTIPLE CHOICE

Circle the letter of the best answer for each question.

1. How are birds and reptiles alike?

a. Both have horny beaks.

b. Both have feathers and wings.

c. Both have scales on their legs and feet.

d. Both have cold bodies.

2. What is the upward force on a flying bird's wings?

a. gravity

b. pressure

c. wind

d. lift

3. How do birds keep their eggs warm?

a. by nesting

b. by brooding

c. by preening

d. by hatching

4. Which of the following is a water bird?

a. robin

b. kiwi

c. blue-footed booby

d. owl

MULTIPLE CHOICE

Circle the letter of the best answer for each question.

5. How do birds of prey use their curved beaks and sharp claws?

a. to build strong nests

b. to catch and eat food

c. to fight enemies

d. to grasp branches

6. What large muscle helps mammals to breathe?

a. rib cage

b. diaphragm

c. air sac

d. mammary gland

7. How does a mammal's brain differ from the brains of other animals of the same size?

a. The mammal's brain is smaller.

b. The mammal's brain is bigger.

c. The mammal's brain is not as complex.

d. The mammal's brain does not stay awake at night.

8. How is a monotreme different from other mammals?

a. A monotreme lays eggs.

b. A monotreme is an endotherm.

c. A monotreme feeds its young milk.

d. A monotreme has a spiny shell.

9. What is the only native North American marsupial?

a. monotreme

b. platypus

c. raccoon

d. opossum

MATCHING

Read the description. Then draw a line from the dot next to each description to the matching word.

10. I have sharp teeth to chew and gnaw. ●

11. I have a small brain and eat insects. ●

12. I am the only flying mammal. ●

13. I am a meat-eater with large canine teeth. ●

a. carnivore

b. bat

c. rodent

d. insectivore

FILL-IN-THE-BLANK

Read the words in the box. Read the sentences. Fill in each blank with the word or phrase that best completes the sentence.

preen	molars
molt	incisors

14. Flat, grinding teeth for chewing are

______________________________.

15. Teeth that cut food are ______________________________.

16. When birds clean and oil their feathers, they

______________________________.

17. When birds lose old feathers and grow new ones, they

______________________________.

placenta	uterus	gestation period

18. In mammals, an embryo grows in the

______________________________.

19. Food and waste are carried between mother and baby by the

______________________________.

20. The time when the embryo develops inside the mother is called the

______________________________.

Name ______________________ Class ____________ Date ____________

Skills Worksheet

Directed Reading B

Section: Everything Is Connected

STUDYING THE WEB OF LIFE

Circle the letter of the best answer for each question.

1. What is the name for the study of interactions of organisms and their environment?

a. population

b. ecology

c. specialization

d. organism

The Two Parts of the Environment

Read the words in the box. Read the sentences. Fill in each blank with the word that best completes the sentence.

abiotic	biotic

2. Alligators and other living organisms are

______________________ parts of the environment.

3. Water, soil, and other nonliving things are

______________________ parts of the environment.

Organization in the Environment

Read the words in the box. Read the sentences. Fill in each blank with the word that best completes the sentence.

ecosystem	individual	population	community

4. The first level of organization is the

______________________ organism.

5. Two or more individuals of the same kind that live together are

a(n) ______________________.

6. All the animals and plants that live in the same place are

a(n) ______________________.

7. A community and its abiotic environment make

a(n) ______________________.

Populations

Circle the letter of the best answer for each question.

8. What are individuals of the same species that live together called?

a. organism
b. sparrows
c. population
d. salt marsh

9. What level of organization are a group of seaside sparrows?

a. community
b. ecosystem
c. population
d. biosphere

Communities

10. What do animals and plants in the same area form?

a. a city
b. a population
c. a community
d. an organism

Ecosystems

Circle the letter of the best answer for each question.

11. What is a community of organisms and the abiotic environment called?

a. individuals

b. ecosystem

c. population

d. community

12. What does an ecologist study in the ecosystem?

a. how rivers are formed

b. how organisms interact

c. only living things

d. only non-living things

The Biosphere

13. What is the biosphere?

a. a group of animals that live together

b. different species of animals in a community

c. the part of Earth where life exists

d. the rivers of a salt marsh

14. Where does the biosphere exist?

a. from deepest ocean to high in the air

b. only from the ocean to Earth's surface

c. only on top of Earth's surface

d. only from Earth's surface to the tops of mountains

Name ______________________ Class ______________ Date ____________

Skills Worksheet

Directed Reading B

Section: Living Things Need Energy

Circle the letter of the best answer for each question.

1. What do all living things need to survive?

a. plants

b. animals

c. organisms

d. energy

THE ENERGY CONNECTION

2. What are the three groups of living things?

a. abiotic, biotic, neutral

b. producers, consumers, decomposers

c. energy, no energy, variable energy

d. grasslands, prairies, water

Producers

Read the words in the box. Read the sentences. Fill in each blank with the word that best completes the sentence.

algae	producers	photosynthesis

3. Organisms that use sunlight to make food

are called ______________________.

4. The process of making sunlight into food

is called ______________________.

5. Plants, ______________________, and some bacteria are producers.

Consumers

Read the description. Then, draw a line from the dot next to each description to the matching word.

6. a consumer that eats only plants ●

7. a consumer that eats only animals ●

8. a consumer that eats both plants and animals ●

9. an omnivore that eats dead things ●

a. herbivore

b. scavenger

c. carnivore

d. omnivore

Decomposers

Circle the letter of the best answer for each question.

10. What are organisms that get energy by breaking down dead organisms called?

a. materials

b. carbon dioxide

c. decomposers

d. water

11. What do decomposers produce?

a. water and carbon dioxide

b. an ecosystem

c. food from sunlight

d. consumers

Name ______________________ Class ______________ Date ____________

Food Chains and Food Webs

<u>Circle the letter</u> of the best answer for each question.

12. What kind of diagram shows how energy flows from one organism to another?

a. producer
c. consumer
b. ecology
d. food chain

13. How is a food web different from a food chain?

a. A food web is smaller.
b. A food web shows more relationships.
c. A food web is simple.
d. A food web has spiders.

14. What are the two main food webs on Earth?

a. animal and plant
b. land and aquatic
c. webs and chains
d. prairie dog and coyote

Energy Pyramids

15. What happens to most of the energy that grass gets from sunlight?

a. The grass stores the energy.
b. The grass feeds prairie dogs.
c. The grass uses the energy to live.
d. The grass gets rid of the energy.

16. What diagram is triangle-shaped and shows how energy is lost?

a. food web
b. food chain
c. energy pyramid
d. community

WOLVES AND THE ENERGY PYRAMID

Circle the letter of the best answer for each question.

17. How can the absence of wolves affect elk populations?

a. the elk eat more animals

b. the elk leave the wilderness

c. the elk overgraze the grass

d. the elk die out

Gray Wolves and the Food Web

18. Why were gray wolves brought back to Yellowstone National Park?

a. to help the elk

b. to restore the natural energy flow

c. to keep the grass from taking over

d. to eat the cows and sheep

Balance in Ecosystems

19. What kind of elk do wolves kill?

a. the strong and healthy

b. the old, injured, and diseased

c. the smart and quick

d. the energetic and fast

Name ______________________ Class ______________ Date ______________

Skills Worksheet

Directed Reading B

Section: Types of Interactions

INTERACTIONS WITH THE ENVIRONMENT

Circle the letter of the best answer for each question.

1. What parts of the environment can control the size of a population?

a. biotic and abiotic factors
b. fish and frogs
c. small ponds
d. seaweed and fish

Limiting Factors

2. Why can't populations grow without stopping?

a. Food and water are limited.
b. Food and water are everywhere.
c. Animals are not strong.
d. Air is limited.

3. What is an example of a limiting factor?

a. when a population is too small
b. when there's not enough food
c. when there's too much food
d. when there's too much water

Carrying Capacity

4. What is the largest population an environment can support called?

a. limiting factors
b. interaction factor
c. population capacity
d. carrying capacity

5. What happens when a population grows larger than its carrying capacity?

a. The population increases more.
b. Individuals die.
c. Individuals grow larger.
d. There is less rainfall.

INTERACTIONS BETWEEN ORGANISMS

Circle the letter of the best answer for each question.

6. What is one of the four ways species affect each other?

a. population
b. competition
c. communities
d. ecology

COMPETITION

7. What is it called when individuals or populations try to use the same resource?

a. cooperation
b. competition
c. capacity
d. community

8. What kind of competition takes place when elks compete for the same food plants?

a. competition between populations
b. competition between communities
c. competition within populations
d. competition within communities

PREDATORS AND PREY

Read the words in the box. Read the sentences. Fill in each blank with the word that best completes the sentence.

predator	prey

9. When a bird eats a worm, the worm is the ______________________.

10. When a bird eats a worm, the bird is the ______________________.

Predator Adaptations

Circle the letter of the best answer for each question.

11. What must predators do to survive?

a. be eaten
b. catch their prey
c. be cheetahs
d. make nests

12. What do cheetahs do to catch prey?

a. hide quietly
b. spin webs
c. run very quickly
d. catch spiders

13. How do goldenrod spiders catch their prey?

a. blend in with the flowers
b. chase insects
c. run very quickly
d. sting insects

Prey Adaptations

14. How do fire salamanders save themselves from predators?

a. spray poison
b. hide in flowers
c. run fast
d. run into burrows

15. What do prairie dogs do to save themselves from predators?

a. hide in flowers
b. catch the predators
c. run into burrows
d. have bright colors

Camouflage

16. What is blending in with the background called?

a. avoidance
b. camouflage
c. community
d. color

17. How do walking stick insects camouflage themselves?

a. build stick houses
b. look like twigs or sticks
c. look like stones
d. freeze against a shrub

Defensive Chemicals

Circle the letter of the best answer for each question.

18. How do the skunks and bombardier beetle save themselves?

a. camouflage and hide

b. run fast

c. spray irritating chemicals

d. freeze against shrubs

Warning Coloration

19. How does an animal advertise that it has a chemical defense?

a. It makes a lot of noise.

b. It tries to look innocent.

c. It stays near other similar animals.

d. It has warning colors like bright red.

SYMBIOSIS

20. What is symbiosis?

a. a distant interaction

b. a close, long-term interaction

c. a close, short-term interaction

d. a chemical interaction

Mutualism

Read the description. Then, draw a line from the dot next to each description to the matching word.

21. a symbiotic relationship in which both organisms benefit ●

22. a living thing that eats food produced by algae ●

23. a living thing that lives in your intestines ●

a. coral

b. bacteria

c. mutualism

Commensalism

Circle the letter of the best answer for each question.

24. In what symbiotic relationship does one living thing benefit while the other is not affected?

a. mutualism

b. camouflage

c. ecosystem

d. commensalism

25. How do sharks and remoras show commensalism?

a. Remoras ride on sharks.

b. Remoras eat sharks.

c. Sharks eat remoras.

d. Remoras save sharks.

Parasitism

Read the words in the box. Read the sentences. Fill in each blank with the word that best completes the sentence.

symbiosis	parasite	host

26. Parasitism is ______________________________ in which one organism benefits and the other is harmed.

27. A parasite gets nourishment from its ______________________________.

28. The host is weakened by the ______________________________.

COEVOLUTION

Circle the letter of the best answer for each question.

29. What is long-term change caused by close interaction of two species called?

a. mutualism

b. parasitism

c. coevolution

d. commensalism

30. How does coevolution affect two species?

a. They eat each other.

b. They change with each other.

c. They use camouflage.

d. They harm each other.

31. How have acacia trees changed through coevolution with ants?

a. They developed ways to fight predators.

b. They developed ways to eat extra ants.

c. They changed by growing taller.

d. They developed structures that make food for ants.

Coevolution and Flowers

32. What is an organism that carries pollen from one flower to another called?

a. a pollinator

b. a polluter

c. a floral

d. a flagellum

32. How did bats change over time to help them spread pollen for flowers?

a. They developed long tongues and noses to reach nectar.

b. They learned to like sugar.

c. They began to eat flowers.

d. Their vision got better.

Name ______________________ Class ______________ Date ____________

Assessment

Chapter Test C

Interactions of Living Things

MULTIPLE CHOICE

Circle the letter of the best answer for each question.

1. Rocks, temperature, and water are what kind of things?

a. biotic

b. abiotic

c. population

d. living

2. What level of organization comes after population?

a. biosphere

b. organism

c. community

d. ecosystem

3. What word describes a community of organisms and their environment?

a. individuals

b. ecosystem

c. population

d. community

4. What living things make food from sunlight?

a. consumers

b. parasites

c. decomposers

d. producers

Circle the letter of the best answer for each question.

5. What happened to other living things when the wolves no longer lived in Yellowstone?

a. They were better off.

b. They were out of balance.

c. They died.

d. They were not changed.

6. When is food a limiting factor?

a. when a population is large

b. when there's too much food

c. when a population is small

d. when there's too much water

7. What is an animal that catches and eats another animal called?

a. prey

b. predator

c. producer

d. herbivore

8. In which relationship do living things help each other?

a. parasitism

b. mutualism

c. organism

d. predator

MATCHING

Read the description. Then, draw a line from the dot next to each description to the matching word.

9. a bear that eats plants and animals

10. a triangle-shaped diagram that shows how energy is lost

11. a type of symbiosis where the host is harmed

12. the area from the oceans to the air where there is life

a. energy pyramid

b. omnivore

c. biosphere

d. parasitism

FILL-IN-THE-BLANK

Read the words in the box. Read the sentences. Fill in each blank with the word or phrase that best completes the sentence.

food chain	food web	producers	omnivores

13. A food web shows energy connections better than a(n) ______________________.

14. Animals that eat plants or animals are ______________________.

15. Living things that make their own food from sunlight are ______________________.

16. A diagram showing the feeding relationships between living things in an ecosystem is a(n) ______________________.

population	biotic	abiotic	community

17. A river carrying nutrients is a(n) ______________________ factor that helps the ecosystem.

18. Plants, animals, and all living things are ______________________ factors.

19. Two or more individuals of the same kind living together are a(n) ______________________.

20. All the populations of living things in the same place are a(n) ______________________.

Name ______________________ Class ______________ Date ______________

Skills Worksheet

Directed Reading B

Section: The Cycles of Matter

THE WATER CYCLE

Circle the letter of the best answer for the question.

1. In the water cycle, where does water move?

a. only between the oceans and the mountains

b. only between the atmosphere and land

c. between the environment and all living things

d. only between plants and animals

How Water Moves

Read the description. Then draw a line from the dot next to each description to the matching letter on the picture.

2. precipitation ●

3. transpiration ●

4. evaporation ●

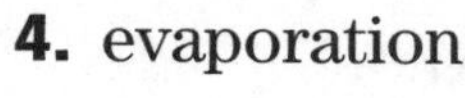

5. condensation ●

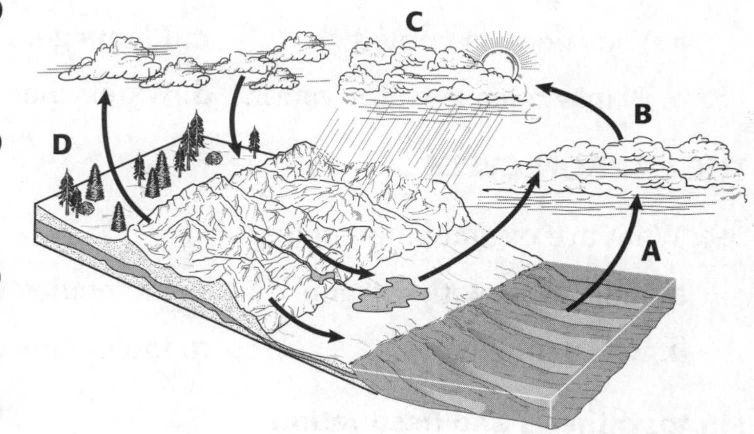

Read the words in the box. Read the sentences. Fill in each blank with the word or phrase that best completes the sentence.

runoff	groundwater

6. The precipitation that falls on land and then into rivers and lakes is called ______________________.

7. Precipitation that is stored in the ground is ______________________.

Water and Life

Circle the letter of the best answer for each question.

8. What happens in the process called transpiration?
   - **a.** Your body is cooled.
   - **b.** Plants release water vapor.
   - **c.** Plants get nutrients.
   - **d.** Water changes to vapor.

THE CARBON CYCLE

9. What are organic molecules?
   - **a.** molecules with oxygen
   - **b.** water molecules
   - **c.** molecules with carbon
   - **d.** molecules of living things

Photosynthesis and Respiration

10. Plants use carbon dioxide to make sugars. What is this process called?
    - **a.** respiration
    - **b.** carbon cycle
    - **c.** photosynthesis
    - **d.** precipitation

11. Which one of the following describes respiration?
    - **a.** releases carbon dioxide
    - **b.** basis of the carbon cycle
    - **c.** makes sugars in plants
    - **d.** keeps carbon in plants

Decomposition and Combustion

Read the words in the box. Read the sentences. Fill in each blank with the word or phrase that best completes the sentence.

combustion	decomposition

12. Breaking down matter into simpler molecules is called

______________________________.

13. Burning matter such as fossil fuels

is called ______________________________.

THE NITROGEN CYCLE

Circle the letter of the best answer for each question.

14. Why is nitrogen important for living things?

a. It helps them use water.
b. It releases carbon dioxide.
c. It helps build new cells.
d. It cools the body.

Converting Nitrogen Gas

15. Which one of the following performs most nitrogen fixation?

a. plants
b. animals
c. bacteria
d. soil

Passing It On

16. What does decomposition do in the nitrogen cycle?

a. changes nitrogen to gas
b. puts nitrogen into soil
c. puts nitrogen into the air
d. gets rid of bacteria

MANY CYCLES

17. Which one of the following statements is true?

a. Only water has a cycle.
b. Each cycle is connected.
c. Matter is not reused.
d. Animals have no role in cycles.

Name ______________________ Class ______________ Date ____________

Skills Worksheet

Directed Reading B

Section: Ecological Succession

Circle the letter of the best answer for each question.

1. Which one of the following describes most trees in Yellowstone National Park right after the 1988 fires?

a. unharmed

b. only ashes left

c. growing again

d. dead but standing

REGROWTH OF A FOREST

2. What was the burned forest of Yellowstone National Park like after 10 years?

a. unchanged

b. growing back

c. fully grown

d. ruined forever

3. Which one of the following statements is an example of succession?

a. A forest burns down.

b. A forest grows back over time.

c. People move into forests.

d. A community becomes a forest.

PRIMARY SUCCESSION

Circle the letter of the best answer for each question.

4. Which one of the following statements describes an area where primary succession can take place?

a. It has lots of soil.

b. It has many trees.

c. It has lakes or ponds.

d. It is bare rock.

5. What term describes the first organisms to live in an area?

a. a community

b. primary succession

c. mosses

d. pioneer species

6. What happens in primary succession?

a. A community builds over time.

b. A forest turns to bare rock.

c. An area is permanently covered with ice.

d. A ruined area grows back.

7. An area of bare rock can become a forest. How long does this take?

a. 100 years

b. a few decades

c. 10 years

d. thousands of years

SECONDARY SUCCESSION

Circle the letter of the best answer for each question.

8. In which area would secondary succession take place?

a. an area of bare rock

b. an unused field

c. a glacier

d. a field of crops

9. What grows first in secondary succession?

a. conifers

b. hardwoods

c. crops

d. weeds

MATURE COMMUNITIES AND BIODIVERSITY

10. What term describes a mature species that has adapted to an area?

a. mature community

b. biodiversity

c. secondary succession

d. climax species

11. A forest has many different kinds of plants and animals. What is this an example of?

a. climax species

b. secondary succession

c. biodiversity

d. primary succession

Name ______________________ Class ______________ Date ______________

Assessment

Chapter Test C

Cycles in Nature

MULTIPLE CHOICE

Circle the letter of the best answer for each question.

1. What do all organic molecules contain?

a. oxygen
b. nitrogen
c. water
d. carbon

2. Why do living things need nitrogen?

a. to build new cells
b. to get rid of wastes
c. to cool them off
d. to carry nutrients

3. Where can primary succession begin?

a. in a place with only rocks
b. in a place with trees
c. in a place with crops
d. in a place with weeds

4. What plant will most likely grow first in secondary succession?

a. pine tree
b. lichen
c. crab grass
d. hardwood tree

5. Which of these might be a climax species?

a. the first species in an area
b. the first insects to eat lichen
c. the most common weeds in a farm field
d. the oldest trees in a forest

MATCHING

Read the description. Then, <u>draw a line</u> from the dot next to each description to the matching word.

6. Bacteria in soil change nitrogen gas into other forms. ●

7. Carbon moves between the environment and living things. ●

8. Nitrogen moves between the environment and living things. ●

9. Plants use carbon dioxide to make sugars. ●

a. photosynthesis

b. nitrogen fixation

c. carbon cycle

d. nitrogen cycle

---

10. A substance burns. ●

11. Plants release water vapor. ●

12. Plants use oxygen and release carbon dioxide. ●

13. A substance is broken into simpler molecules. ●

a. respiration

b. transpiration

c. combustion

d. decomposition

FILL-IN-THE-BLANK

Read the words in the box. Read the sentences. Fill in each blank with the word or phrase that best completes the sentence.

runoff	biodiversity	pioneer species
succession	groundwater	

14. Precipitation that is stored in the ground is

______________________________.

15. The growing of a community over time is

______________________________.

16. The variety of species present in an area is called

______________________________.

17. Precipitation that runs from land to rivers and lakes is

______________________________.

18. The first living things to grow in an area are

______________________________.

MATCHING

Read the description. Then, draw a line from the dot next to each description to the matching letter on the picture.

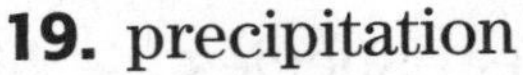

19. precipitation ●

20. transpiration ●

21. evaporation ●

22. condensation ●

Name ______________________ Class ______________ Date ____________

Skills Worksheet

Directed Reading B

Section: Land Biomes

THE EARTH'S LAND BIOMES

Read the words in the box. Read the sentences. Fill in each blank with the word or phrase that best completes the sentence.

biome	biotic	abiotic

1. Parts of an environment that are alive are

______________________ factors.

2. An area with a certain climate and certain plants and animals is

a(n) ______________________.

3. Parts of an environment that are not alive, such as soil and climate,

are ______________________ factors.

FORESTS

Temperate Deciduous Forests

Circle the letter of the best answer for each question.

4. What does the word *deciduous* mean?

a. "to change color"

b. "to fall off"

c. "to decide"

d. "to change seasons"

5. Why do deciduous trees lose their leaves?

a. to feed animals

b. to make the soil better

c. to save water during winter

d. to get more sunlight

Coniferous Forests

Circle the letter of the best answer for each question.

6. Where are conifer seeds produced?

a. in cones

b. in waxy leaves

c. in needles

d. in trunks

7. What covers the needles of conifers?

a. sap

b. bark

c. weeds

d. waxy coating

8. Why do few large plants grow beneath conifers?

a. It is too cold.

b. Animals eat them.

c. Little light reaches the ground.

d. The ground is too bare.

Tropical Rain Forests

9. What does *biological diversity* mean?

a. a lot of rain

b. rich soil

c. more kinds of plants and animals

d. great climate differences

10. What is the rain-forest canopy?

a. treetops

b. vines

c. tree trunks

d. ground

GRASSLANDS

Temperate Grasslands

Circle the letter of the best answer for each question.

11. What are the main plants in temperate grasslands?

a. conifers

b. shrubs

c. grasses

d. crops

12. Why don't temperate grasslands have trees?

a. too much rain

b. fires

c. deep roots

d. rolling hills

Savannas

13. What is the climate of a savanna?

a. rainy year-round

b. seasonal rains

c. always dry and hot

d. always cold and wet

DESERTS

14. Which is a way plants adapt to the desert climate?

a. They grow far apart.

b. They grow under the ground.

c. They have roots above the ground.

d. They do not have flowers.

Each description tells how an animal adapts to the desert. Read the description. Then, draw a line from the dot next to each description to the matching word.

15. stores water under its shell ●	**a.** jack rabbit
16. recycles water from its food ●	**b.** spadefoot toad
17. big ears get rid of body heat ●	**c.** desert tortoise
18. buries self during dry season ●	**d.** kangaroo rat

TUNDRA

Circle the letter of the best answer for each question.

19. Which describes tundra?

a. cold temperatures and much rain

b. warm temperatures and seasonal rain

c. cold temperatures and little rain

d. cold winter and hot summers

Polar Tundra

20. What is permafrost?

a. soil that has thawed

b. soil that is always frozen

c. a plant in the tundra

d. muddy soil

Alpine Tundra

21. How does alpine tundra differ from polar tundra?

a. It does not have permafrost

b. It gets no sunlight.

c. It is on mountain tops.

d. It has many trees.

Name ________________ Class ________ Date ________

Skills Worksheet

Directed Reading B

Section: Marine Ecosystems

LIFE IN THE OCEAN

Circle the letter of the best answer for each question.

1. Which describes the animals in the marine ecosystem?

a. large animals
b. small animals
c. tiny and huge animals
d. no animals

2. Why are plankton important to the marine ecosystem?

a. They are very tiny.
b. They are food for many animals.
c. They do not need sunlight.
d. They can float.

TEMPERATURE

3. How does the temperature of ocean water change as it gets deeper?

a. It gets warmer.
b. It gets colder.
c. It stays the same.
d. It gets colder and then warmer.

4. Which ocean zone has the warmest water?

a. deep zone
b. thermocline
c. surface zone
d. middle layer

5. Which animals have adapted to near-freezing water?

a. barnacles
b. animals in coral reefs
c. fishes in polar areas
d. whales

DEPTH AND SUNLIGHT

The Intertidal Zone

6. What must animals in the intertidal zone adapt to?

a. cold water
b. exposure to air
c. hot water
d. deep water

The Neritic Zone

Circle the letter of the best answer for each question.

7. Which describes the ocean floor in the neritic zone?

a. flat
b. has bumps
c. has cracks
d. slopes downward

The Oceanic Zone

8. Which describes the oceanic zone?

a. where ocean meets land
b. no sunlight
c. few animals
d. has very deep water

The Benthic Zone

9. How do many animals in the benthic zone get their food?

a. They eat plankton.
b. They get food that sinks from above.
c. They eat animals on shore.
d. They make it from sunlight.

A CLOSER LOOK

10. How does the ocean provide Earth's precipitation?

a. through its temperatures
b. through evaporation
c. through wind patterns
d. through its ecosystems

Intertidal Areas

11. Which is an intertidal area?

a. coral reef
b. rocky shore
c. pond
d. swamp

Coral Reefs

Circle the letter of the best answer for each question.

12. What are coral reefs made up of?

a. algae

b. skeletons of corals

c. sea stars

d. sea urchins

Estuaries

13. Which of the following describes an estuary?

a. a place where fresh water and salt water mix

b. a place that is poor in nutrients

c. a place with high salt concentrations

d. a place with few plankton

The Sargasso Sea

14. Which of the following is a characteristic of the Sargasso Sea?

a. It has no plant life.

b. It has big rafts of algae.

c. It is red in color.

d. It has no animals.

Polar Ice

15. Which of the following describes the polar ice ecosystem?

a. The ice has few nutrients.

b. No large animals live there.

c. It is too cold for animals.

d. Plankton provides food for animals.

Name ______________________ Class ______________ Date ____________

Skills Worksheet

Directed Reading B

Section: Freshwater Ecosystems

STREAM AND RIVER ECOSYSTEMS

Circle the letter of the best answer for each question.

1. Where does water in a river come from?

a. the ocean or a sea
b. melting snow or a spring
c. a delta or a stream
d. intertidal areas

2. What is an important abiotic factor in freshwater ecosystems?

a. how many plants there are
b. how many fish there are
c. how animals have adapted
d. how fast water moves

Each description tells how a plant or animal adapts in moving water. Read the description. Then, draw a line from the dot next to each description to the matching word.

3. attach to rocks	●	**a.** insects
4. live under rocks	●	**b.** tadpoles
5. use suction disks	●	**c.** algae and moss

POND AND LAKE ECOSYSTEMS

Life near Shore

Circle the letter of the best answer for each question.

6. Where is the littoral zone of a lake located?

a. close to the edge
b. in the middle
c. at the bottom
d. above the water

Life Away from Shore

7. What lives in the open-water zone of a lake?

a. snakes
b. clams and worms
c. crustaceans
d. fishes

Circle the letter of the best answer for each question.

8. Which describes the deep-water zone?

a. It gets a lot of sunlight.

b. It gets no sunlight.

c. No fish live there.

d. Cattails and rushes grow there.

WETLAND ECOSYSTEMS

9. Which of the following is a characteristic of a wetland?

a. Animals cannot live there.

b. They help control floods.

c. They are good to build on.

d. They have fast-moving water.

Marshes

10. Which of the following describes marshes?

a. an area with many trees

b. an area with no animals

c. found in shallow areas near shores

d. an area with few grasses or reeds

Swamps

11. How do swamps differ from marshes?

a. Swamps are near rivers.

b. Swamps have many birds.

c. Swamps are very wet.

d. Swamps have trees.

FROM A LAKE TO A FOREST

Read the description. Then, draw a line from the dot next to each description to the matching word.

12. decompose dead leaves and animals in a pond •

13. fills a lake or pond over time •

14. what a lake becomes as it fills and plants begin to grow toward the center •

15. eventually, a filled-in lake will dry out and become this •

a. forest

b. sediment

c. bacteria

d. wetland

Name ______________________ Class ______________ Date ____________

Assessment

Chapter Test C

The Earth's Ecosystems

MULTIPLE CHOICE

Circle the letter of the best answer for each question.

1. What is permafrost?

a. dry desert soil

b. muddy soil

c. ice on the tundra

d. soil that is always frozen

2. Which is a key abiotic factor in rivers?

a. number of fish

b. speed of water

c. amount of salt

d. how animals adapt

3. Which ocean animals need warm water to live?

a. whales

b. barnacles

c. animals on the ocean floor

d. animals on coral reefs

4. How does a swamp differ from a marsh?

a. It has salt water.

b. It has trees.

c. It has many birds.

d. It has very wet soil.

Circle the letter of the best answer for each question.

5. Which ocean temperature zone is the warmest?

a. surface zone

b. thermocline

c. deep zone

d. littoral zone

6. Which of the following is NOT an intertidal area?

a. sandy beach

b. coral reef

c. rocky shore

d. mudflat

7. Many animals live in the polar ice ecosystem. What makes this possible?

a. cold air

b. large numbers of plankton

c. floating algae

d. coral reefs

8. Which lake zone is closest to the land's edge?

a. open-water zone

b. deep-water zone

c. littoral zone

d. tributary

MATCHING

Read the description. Then, draw a line from the dot next to each description to the matching term.

9. has the greatest biological diversity of any land biome	●	**a.** temperate grassland
10. has trees with cones	●	**b.** coniferous forest
11. main plants are grasses	●	**c.** alpine tundra
12. found on mountain tops	●	**d.** tropical rain forest

13. the ocean floor	●	**a.** neritic zone
14. where the ocean meets the land	●	**b.** oceanic zone
15. has warm water and sunlight	●	**c.** benthic zone
16. sea floor drops sharply	●	**d.** intertidal zone

FILL-IN-THE-BLANK

Read the words in the box. Read the sentences. Fill in each blank with the word or phrase that best completes the sentence.

swamp	forest	wetland	marsh

17. An important ecosystem for flood control is a

________________________________.

18. A wetland with no trees is a ________________________________.

19. An ecosystem with trees and that is partly under water is a

________________________________.

20. A lake may get filled in with sediment. It may become a wetland and then a ________________________________.

Name ______________________ Class ______________ Date ____________

Skills Worksheet

Directed Reading B

Section: Environmental Problems

POLLUTION

Circle the letter of the best answer for each question.

1. Five major kinds of pollutants are chemicals, noise, garbage, gases, and what else?
   - **a.** radiation
   - **b.** solar wastes
   - **c.** renewable resources
   - **d.** biodegradable wastes

2. Which of the following is an unwanted change in the environment caused by harmful substances?
   - **a.** overpopulation
   - **b.** biodiversity
   - **c.** pollution
   - **d.** evolution

Garbage

3. Who throws away the most trash?
   - **a.** animals
   - **b.** average Americans
   - **c.** people in other nations
   - **d.** exotic species

4. What kind of wastes can catch fire, explode, or make people sick?
   - **a.** harmful wastes
   - **b.** dangerous wastes
   - **c.** hazardous wastes
   - **d.** critical wastes

Chemicals

Circle the letter of the best answer for each question.

5. What might some chemicals do to the environment?

a. They might harm the environment.

b. They might increase the environment.

c. They might burn the environment.

d. They might renew the environment.

6. What are two harmful chemicals that are now banned?

a. ozone and fertilizers

b. PCBs and ozone

c. fertilizers and CFCs

d. CFCs and PCBs

7. Which of the following types of chemicals destroy the ozone that protects people from harmful ultraviolet light?

a. pesticides

b. CFCs

c. PCBs

d. fertilizers

High-Powered Wastes

8. What dangerous wastes are produced by nuclear power plants?

a. chemical wastes

b. radioactive wastes

c. poisonous gas

d. harmful paints

Gases

9. Which of the following air pollutants has increased since the Industrial Revolution?

a. oxygen

b. carbon dioxide

c. hydrogen

d. ultraviolet light

10. What do some scientists think more carbon dioxide in the atmosphere has caused?

a. more rain

b. more clouds

c. higher global temperatures

d. longer winters

Circle the letter of the best answer for each question.

11. If higher global temperatures melted the polar icecaps, what could happen?

a. coastal floods
b. colder air
c. less rain
d. more rain

Noise

12. Which of the following does noise pollution damage?

a. the atmosphere
b. your hearing
c. the ocean
d. the land

RESOURCE DEPLETION

Read the description. Then, draw a line from the dot next to each description to the matching words.

13. a resource that can be used over or has an unlimited supply ●

14. a resource that cannot last forever ●

a. nonrenewable resource

b. renewable resource

Renewable or Nonrenewable?

Circle the letter of the best answer for each question.

15. What might happen if fresh water is used faster than it can be replaced?

a. Plants and animals will survive without water.
b. People might drink less water.
c. Fresh water might run out.
d. Nothing will happen to the water.

EXOTIC SPECIES

16. What are organisms that make homes in new places called?

a. strange species
b. exotic species
c. endangered species
d. new species

Circle the letter of the best answer for each question.

17. Why do some exotic animal species harm new habitats?

a. They don't have predators.

b. They don't have prey.

c. They can't build nests.

d. They can't find food.

HUMAN POPULATION GROWTH

18. What kind of advances have helped the human population grow?

a. advances in computers and television

b. advances in housing and clothing

c. advances in medicine and farming

d. advances in education and entertainment

19. The presence of too many individuals in an area for the available resources is called what?

a. crowding

b. overpopulation

c. migration

d. concentration

HABITAT DESTRUCTION

20. What do we call the number and variety of organisms living together in an area?

a. families

b. species

c. biodiversity

d. kingdoms

Read the words in the box. Read the sentences. Fill in each blank with the word or phrase that best completes the sentence.

biodiversity	habitat

21. The place where an organism lives is called

a(n) ______________________________.

22. When a habitat is damaged or destroyed,

______________________________ is lost.

Forest Habitats

Circle the letter of the best answer for each question.

23. What is deforestation?

a. the planting of forests
b. the animals in the forest
c. the clearing of forest lands
d. the trees in the forest

Marine Habitats

24. What is pollution that comes from only one source called?

a. point-source pollution
b. nonpoint-source pollution
c. harmful pollution
d. one-source pollution

25. What is pollution that comes from many different sources called?

a. point-source pollution
b. nonpoint-source pollution
c. harmful pollution
d. many-source pollution

Circle the letter of the best answer for each question.

26. When harmful chemicals are dumped into marine habitats, what might happen?

a. The chemicals might kill or harm marine organisms.

b. The chemicals might dry up the water.

c. The chemicals might cause flooding.

d. The chemicals might cause deforestation.

EFFECTS ON HUMANS

27. When something in the environment harms other organisms, what will also be harmed?

a. travel

b. communication

c. rocks

d. people

28. What disease might chemicals cause years after someone is exposed to them?

a. chicken pox

b. cancer

c. measles

d. colds

Name ______________________ Class ______________ Date ____________

Skills Worksheet

Directed Reading B

Section: Environmental Solutions

CONSERVATION

Circle the letter of the best answer for each question.

1. What is the preservation and wise use of natural resources?

a. recycling

b. biodiversity

c. conservation

d. ecology

2. When someone practices conservation, what do they use fewer of?

a. muscles

b. food

c. natural resources

d. trees

3. Which is NOT one of the three Rs of conservation?

a. reuse

b. recycle

c. reduce

d. rebuild

REDUCE

4. What is the best way to conserve Earth's natural resources?

a. use more of the resources

b. use the resources in different ways

c. use less of the resources

d. make more resources

Reducing Waste and Pollution

5. What kind of waste can be broken down by living organisms?

a. biodegradable waste

b. thin waste

c. aluminum waste

d. light weight waste

Circle the letter of the best answer for each question.

6. What are some farmers doing to help protect the environment?

a. planting fewer acres

b. watering fields more often

c. practicing organic farming

d. using chemical fertilizers

Reducing Use of Nonrenewable Resources

7. What do some homes now use for power instead of burning fossil fuels?

a. natural gas

b. oil

c. solar energy

d. coal

8. What do electric cars produce less of?

a. fossil fuels

b. pollution

c. energy

d. gasoline

REUSE

9. What are you doing if you fix something instead of throwing it away?

a. You are reusing it.

b. You are recycling it.

c. You are remixing it.

d. You are reducing it.

Reusing Products

Read the description. Then, draw a line from the dot next to each description to the matching words.

10. can be used in new buildings ●

11. can be used to make playground surfaces ●

12. can be used to make park benches ●

a. old tires

b. old wood

c. plastic bags

Reusing Water

Circle the letter of the best answer for each question.

13. Which of the following is a way to use reclaimed water?

a. drink it

b. put it in bottles

c. water plants with it

d. put fish in it

RECYCLE

14. What is the recovery of materials from waste called?

a. recycling

b. reusing

c. renewing

d. reducing

Recycling Trash

15. What can recycling newspapers do?

a. save millions of trees

b. save bottles and jars

c. make new tires

d. make more plastics

16. What can be made out of recycled glass?

a. fertilizer

b. newspapers

c. new bottles and jars

d. park benches

Recycling Resources

17. What is using garbage to make electricity called?

a. a waste of electricity

b. recycled energy

c. resource depletion

d. resource recovery

MAINTAINING BIODIVERSITY

Circle the letter of the best answer for each question.

18. Why is maintaining biodiversity important?

a. because biodiversity uses resources

b. because biodiversity uses up land

c. because biodiversity helps the environment

d. because biodiversity destroys habitats

19. Which of the following does NOT maintain biodiversity?

a. growing a variety of plants on a farm

b. protecting all the species in an ecosystem

c. protecting the habitats in an ecosystem

d. removing an important predator from an ecosystem

Read the description. Then, draw a line from the dot next to each description to the matching words.

20. a way to protect entire habitats ●

21. a law that protects some individual species ●

22. a way to increase the population of an endangered species ●

a. nature preserves

b. recovery programs

c. the Endangered Species Act

ENVIRONMENTAL STRATEGIES

Circle the letter of the best answer for each question.

23. Besides reducing pesticide use, what is another environmental strategy?

a. drinking less water

b. increasing deforestation

c. putting wastes on farmland

d. developing alternative energy sources

Circle the letter of the best answer for each question.

24. What government organization was formed to help protect the environment?

a. the Endangered Species Act

b. the Wildlife Foundation

c. the National Environment Association

d. the Environmental Protection Agency

WHAT YOU CAN DO

25. What is NOT a way for people to help protect the environment?

a. buying products made from endangered species

b. volunteering at a nature preserve

c. using rechargeable batteries

d. buying products made from recycled materials

26. What can you do with waste glass, plastics, paper, and aluminum to protect the environment?

a. burn them

b. put them in a landfill

c. recycle them

d. repair them

Name ______________________ Class ______________ Date ______________

Assessment

Chapter Test C

Environmental Problems and Solutions

MULTIPLE CHOICE

Circle the letter of the best answer for each question.

1. Aside from gases, noise, garbage, and radioactive wastes, what is another kind of pollution?

a. deforestation

b. chemicals

c. biodiversity

d. exotic species

2. Which of the following is an unwanted change in the environment that is caused by harmful substances?

a. conservation

b. garbage

c. nonrenewable resources

d. pollution

3. What is an organism's home called?

a. a habitat

b. an environment

c. a house

d. a neighborhood

4. What is lost when habitats are damaged or destroyed?

a. biodiversity

b. fossil fuels

c. exotic species

d. pollutants

5. What are some farmers doing to help the environment?

a. not planting crops

b. practicing organic farming

c. watering their crops more

d. watering their crops less

Circle the letter of the best answer for each question.

6. What kinds of advances have helped the human population grow?

a. advances in transportation and electronics

b. advances in TV and radio

c. advances in medicine and farming

d. advances in housing and education

7. What organisms make homes for themselves in new places?

a. predator species

b. animal species

c. endangered species

d. exotic species

8. If rising global temperatures melt the polar caps, what might happen to coastal areas?

a. more clouds

b. deeper oceans

c. more rain

d. more flooding

9. How are electric cars good for the environment?

a. They use more fossil fuels.

b. They produce less energy.

c. They produce less pollution.

d. They use more gasoline.

10. Which of the following is an important environmental strategy?

a. drinking less water

b. using pesticides

c. adopting stray animals

d. protecting habitats

MATCHING

Read the description. Then, <u>draw a line</u> from the dot next to each description to the matching word.

11. This environmental strategy includes recycling and buying recycled products. ●	**a.** developing alternative energy sources
12. This environmental strategy includes asking the government to protect endangered species. ●	**b.** enforcing the Endangered Species Act
13. This environmental strategy includes using solar and wind power. ●	**c.** reducing pollution

---

14. recovering materials from waste ●	**a.** reducing
15. fixing something instead of throwing it away ●	**b.** recycling
16. using fewer natural resources ●	**c.** reusing

FILL-IN-THE-BLANK

Read the words in the box. Read the sentences. Fill in each blank with the word or phrase that best completes the sentence.

biodiversity	renewable resource	nonrenewable resource
conservation	overpopulation	pollutant

17. Anything that causes pollution is a(n)

______________________.

18. A resource that cannot last forever is

a(n) ______________________.

19. A resource that can be used over and over is

a(n) ______________________.

20. The number and variety of organisms living in an area is

called ______________________.

21. The presence of more individuals in an area than the area can

support is called ______________________.

22. The wise use and preservation of natural resources is

called ______________________.

Name ______________________ Class ______________ Date ____________

Skills Worksheet

Directed Reading B

Section: Body Organization

Circle the letter of the best answer for each question.

1. What does homeostasis do in the body?

a. keeps the body stable

b. keeps the body unstable

c. makes the body shiver all of the time

d. keeps the body cold

CELLS, TISSUES, AND ORGANS

2. What can happen if homeostasis is disrupted?

a. Cells rest.

b. Cells work together.

c. Cells may be hurt or die.

d. Cells remove waste.

3. What is a group of cells that are alike and work together?

a. a cell team

b. a tissue

c. a cell family

d. a system

Read the description. Then, draw a line from the dot next to each description to the matching word.

4. holds organs together	●	**a.** nervous tissue
5. covers and protects tissue	●	**b.** muscle tissue
6. sends messages to parts of the body	●	**c.** epithelial tissue
7. helps you move	●	**d.** connective tissue

Tissues Form Organs

Read the words in the box. Read the sentences. Fill in each blank with the word or phrase that best completes the sentence.

muscle tissue	organ	epithelial tissue
nervous tissue	organ system	

8. A group of tissues that work together is a(n)

______________________________.

9. The stomach uses ______________________________ to break up food.

10. Your stomach's ______________________________ tells your body you are full after eating.

11. The inside of your stomach is covered with

______________________________.

Organs Form Systems

12. Organs that work together are part of a(n)

______________________________.

WORKING TOGETHER

Circle the letter of the best answer for the question.

13. How do the circulatory and cardiovascular systems help maintain homeostasis?

a. They support the body.

b. They deliver materials.

c. They store wastes.

d. They include the heart, blood, and vessels.

Read the description. Then, draw a line from the dot next to each description to the matching word.

14. includes the heart and blood vessels	**a.** cardiovascular system
15. takes wastes out of blood	**b.** endocrine system
16. sends chemical messages	**c.** integumentary system
17. includes skin, hair, and nails	**d.** urinary system

18. makes sperm	**a.** skeletal system
19. holds up and protects parts of the body	**b.** lymphatic system
20. gets rid of bacteria and viruses	**c.** male reproductive system
21. takes oxygen from the air and releases carbon dioxide	**d.** respiratory system

22. breaks down food into substances the body can use	**a.** female reproductive system
23. helps the body move	**b.** digestive system
24. protects the fetus	**c.** nervous system
25. sends and receives electrical messages	**d.** muscular system

Name ______________________ Class ____________ Date __________

Skills Worksheet

Directed Reading B

Section: The Skeletal System

Read the words in the box. Read the sentences. Fill in each blank with the word that best completes the sentence.

minerals	cartilage	ribs
movement	marrow	

1. Your skeletal system is made up of bones, connective tissue, and

______________________.

BONES

2. Your muscles pull on your bones to cause

______________________.

3. Your ______________________ protect your heart and lungs.

4. Bones store ______________________ and fat.

5. Some bones are filled with ______________________, which makes blood cells.

Bone Structure

Circle the letter of the best answer for the question.

6. What words describe compact bone?

a. soft and moist

b. hard and dense

c. dry and brittle

b. round and hollow

Circle the letter of the best answer for each question.

7. What does spongy bone have a lot of?

a. blood vessels

b. dead cells

c. water

d. open spaces

8. What can you find inside compact bone?

a. small blood vessels

b. open spaces

c. marrow

d. soft tissue

9. What kind of bone tissue gives bones most of their strength and support?

a. compact bone

b. spongy bone

c. red marrow

d. yellow marrow

Draw a line from each term to the matching number on the picture.

spongy bone   compact bone   blood vessels

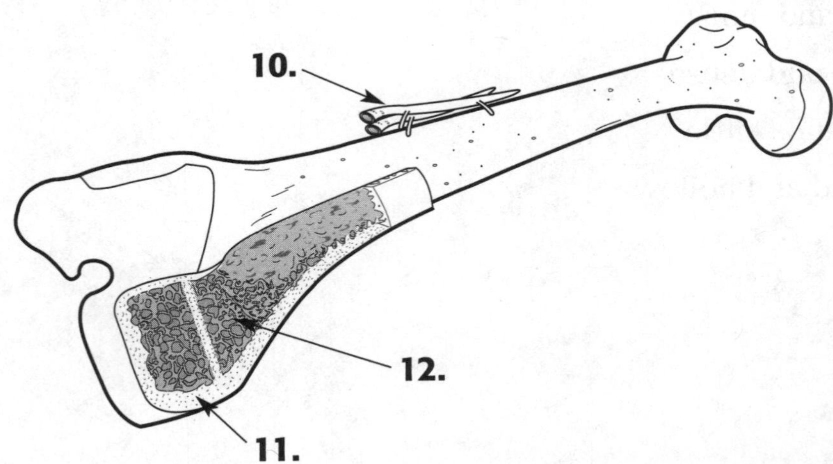

Bone Growth

Circle the letter of the best answer for each question.

13. What is most of your skeleton made of when you are born?

a. marrow

b. compact bone

c. cartilage

d. spongy bone

JOINTS

Read the description. Then, draw a line from the dot next to each description to the matching word.

14. lets you straighten and bend your leg •

15. lets you move your arm all around •

16. lets you move your wrist •

a. gliding joint

b. hinge joint

c. ball-and-socket joint

---

17. the place where two or more bones meet •

18. pads the place where two or more bones meet •

19. band of stretchy tissue that connects bones •

20. type of joint in which bones move very little •

a. ligament

b. fixed joint

c. joint

d. cartilage

SKELETAL SYSTEM INJURIES AND DISEASES

Read the words in the box. Read the sentences. Fill in each blank with the word or phrase that best completes the sentences.

sprain	arthritis	fracture
osteoporosis	dislocated joint	

21. An injury in which one or more bones have been moved out of place is called a(n) _______________.

22. If a ligament is stretched too far or torn, a(n) _______________ happens.

23. A disease in which bones become weak and soft is called _______________.

24. A disease in which joints hurt and become stiff is called _______________.

25. A broken bone is called a(n) _______________.

Name ______________________ Class ______________ Date ____________

Skills Worksheet

Directed Reading B

Section: The Muscular System

Circle the letter of the best answer for each question.

KINDS OF MUSCLE

1. What part of your body has smooth muscle?

a. digestive tract
b. spinal cord
c. heart
d. skin

2. What part of your body has cardiac muscle?

a. stomach
b. brain
c. heart
d. nose

3. Skeletal muscle is connected to what parts of the body?

a. lungs
b. bones
c. ears
d. eyes

4. What do you call muscle action that you can control?

a. voluntary
b. involuntary
c. light
d. heavy

5. What do you call muscle action that you cannot control?

a. voluntary
b. involuntary
c. light
d. heavy

MOVEMENT

6. What travels from your brain to your skeletal muscle cells when you want to move?

a. tendons
b. contractions
c. connective tissue
d. signals

Muscles Attach to Bones

<u>Circle the letter</u> of the best answer for each question.

7. What structure attaches a skeletal muscle to a bone?

a. cartilage

b. marrow

c. tendon

d. ligament

Muscles Work in Pairs

Read the words in the box. Read the sentences. <u>Fill in each blank</u> with the word that best completes the sentence.

flexor	extensor

8. A muscle that bends part of your body is a(n)

______________________.

9. A muscle that straightens part of your body is a(n)

______________________.

USE IT OR LOSE IT

resistance exercise	endurance
exercise	aerobic exercise

10. To make muscles strong, you must ______________________.

11. Your muscles can work longer if you have more

______________________.

12. Doing ______________________ helps make skeletal muscles stronger.

13. Doing ______________________ helps strengthen the heart.

MUSCLE INJURY

Circle the letter of the best answer for each question.

14. Why is it a good idea to start working out slowly?

a. It is safer.

b. It is more fun.

c. It saves time.

d. It is easier.

15. What happens when a muscle or tendon is overstretched or torn?

a. a sprain

b. a strain

c. tendinitis

d. arthritis

16. What word describes an injured tendon if you have tendinitis?

a. soft

b. torn

c. rested

d. inflamed

17. What drugs do some people take to make muscles stronger?

a. aspirin

b. anabolic steroids

c. antibiotics

d. allergy medicine

18. What is a health problem that can result from taking anabolic steroids?

a. bad vision

b. headaches

c. high blood pressure

d. knee pain

Name ______________________ Class ______________ Date ____________

Skills Worksheet

Directed Reading B

Section: The Integumentary System

Read the words in the box. Read the sentences. Fill in each blank with the word or phrase that best completes the sentence.

skin	integumentary system

1. The largest organ in the body is the ______________________.

2. Skin, hair, and nails make up your ______________________.

FUNCTIONS OF SKIN

wastes	melanin	sweat glands
water	nerve endings	ultraviolet light

3. Skin keeps ______________________ in your body.

4. You can feel things around you through the ______________________ in your skin.

5. Darker skin has more ______________________ than lighter skin.

6. Melanin absorbs ______________________ from the sun to protect your skin.

7. Small organs in the skin called ______________________ make sweat.

8. Sweating helps remove ______________________ from the body.

LAYERS OF SKIN

Circle the letter of the best answer for each question.

9. What is the outside layer of skin called?

a. thin tissue

b. thick tissue

c. dermis

d. epidermis

10. What layer of skin is under the top layer of skin?

a. thin tissue

b. thick tissue

c. dermis

d. epidermis

Epidermis

11. What is the epidermis made of?

a. epithelial tissue

b. nervous tissue

c. connective tissue

d. muscle tissue

12. What protein fills most cells of the epidermis?

a. fat

b. fiber

c. keratin

d. minerals

Name ______________________ Class ______________ Date ____________

Dermis

Circle the letter of the best answer for the question.

13. What protein makes up part of the dermis?

a. collagen

b. oil

c. keratin

d. follicles

Read the description. Then, draw a line from the dot next to each description to the matching word.

14. make hair	**a.** blood vessels
15. transport substances and control body temperature	**b.** nerve fibers
16. carry messages to and from the brain	**c.** hair follicles

17. waterproof the dermis	**a.** muscle fibers
18. help remove waste from the body	**b.** oil glands
19. can cause hair to stand up	**c.** sweat glands

HAIR AND NAILS

Circle the letter of the best answer for each question.

20. What are hair and nails made up of?

a. skin

b. all dead cells

c. all living cells

d. living and dead cells

21. Which of the following statements about hair follicles is true?

a. They have living cells.

b. They make new skin.

c. They have all dead cells.

d. They make new nails.

22. What gives hair its color?

a. new cells

b. water

c. keratin

d. melanin

23. How does hair help your body?

a. draws dust into the skin

b. cools the body

c. protects skin from the sun

d. keeps water in the body

24. What part of a nail has living cells?

a. nail shell

b. nail root

c. nail stem

d. nail base

SKIN INJURIES

Read the words in the box. Read the sentences. Fill in each blank with the word or phrase that best completes the sentence.

blood clot	acne
cancer	bacteria-fighting cells

25. A person can get ______________________ if the genetic material in skin cells is damaged.

26. A person can get ______________________ if too much oil blocks hair follicles.

27. A cut stops bleeding as a(n) ______________________ forms.

28. Cells that kill harmful bacteria are called ______________________.

Name ________________________ Class ______________ Date ______________

Assessment

Chapter Test C

Body Organization and Structure

MULTIPLE CHOICE

Circle the letter of the best answer for each question.

1. What is a group of cells that are alike and work together?

a. a cell team
b. a tissue
c. a cell family
d. a system

2. What kind of bone tissue gives bones strength and support?

a. compact bone
b. spongy bone
c. red marrow
b. yellow marrow

3. What part of your body has cardiac muscle?

a. stomach
b. brain
c. heart
d. nose

4. What kind of injury happens if a muscle is stretched too far?

a. a fracture
b. arthritis
c. a strain
d. tendinitis

5. What is the outside layer of skin called?

a. thin tissue
b. thick tissue
c. dermis
d. epidermis

6. What gives hair its color?

a. new cells
b. collagen
c. keratin
d. melanin

MATCHING

Read the description. Then, draw a line from the dot next to each description to the matching word.

7. frame that holds up and protects parts of the body ●
8. stretchy tissue that connects bones ●
9. structure that lets you move your arm all around ●
10. structure in the skin that helps keep you cool ●

a. ball-and-socket joint
b. sweat glands
c. skeletal system
d. ligaments

---

11. breaks down food so the body can use it ●
12. sends chemical messages ●
13. includes the blood vessels and heart ●
14. takes waste out of the blood ●

a. urinary system
b. cardiovascular system
c. endocrine system
d. digestive system

FILL-IN-THE-BLANK

Read the words in the box. Read the sentences. Fill in each blank with the word or phrase that best completes the sentence.

osteoporosis	flexor
organ	marrow

15. A group of two of more tissues that work together form a(n) ______________________.

16. Bones contain ______________________, which makes blood cells.

17. A disease that makes bones weak and break more easily is called ______________________.

19. You can bend a part of your body with a(n) ______________________ muscle.

MATCHING

Draw a line from each term to the number on the picture.

compact bone spongy bone blood vessels

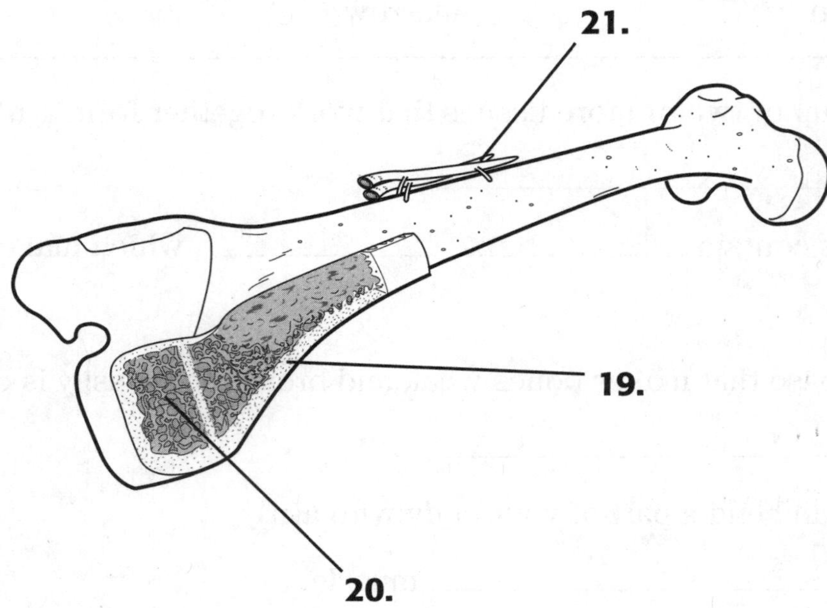

Name ______________________ Class ______________ Date ____________

Skills Worksheet

Directed Reading B

Section: The Cardiovascular System

YOUR CARDIOVASCULAR SYSTEM

Read the words in the box. Read the sentences. Fill in each blank with the word or phrase that best completes the sentence.

blood	blood vessels
cardiovascular system	heart

1. The heart and blood vessels are part of the

______________________.

2. Blood vessels carry ______________________ throughout your body.

3. Blood is pumped by the ______________________.

4. Arteries, capillaries, and veins are types of

______________________.

THE HEART

Circle the letter of the best answer for each question.

5. How many chambers does the heart have?

a. 1

b. 2

c. 3

d. 4

6. What are the heart's upper chambers called?

a. atria

b. ventricles

c. valves

d. cardios

Circle the letter of the best answer for each question.

7. What are the heart's lower chambers called?

a. atria

b. ventricles

c. valves

d. cardios

8. What kind of blood gets sent to the lungs?

a. type A

b. type B

c. oxygen-rich

d. oxygen-poor

9. What kind of blood gets sent to the body?

a. type A

b. oxygen-rich

c. type B

d. oxygen-poor

10. What causes the sound of a heartbeat?

a. atria contracting

b. valves closing

c. ventricles contracting

d. atria relaxing

BLOOD VESSELS

Read the words in the box. Read the sentences. Fill in each blank with the word or phrase that best completes the sentence.

capillaries	arteries	blood vessels
veins	pulse	

11. Blood vessels that carry blood from the heart are

______________________.

12. Blood vessels that allow exchanges between blood and cells are

______________________.

13. Blood vessels that carry blood to the heart are

______________________.

14. Your ______________________ is caused by rhythmic changes in your blood pressure.

15. Blood travels through your body in hollow tubes called

______________________.

TWO TYPES OF CIRCULATION

Read the description. Then, draw a line from the dot next to each description to the matching word.

16. flow of blood between heart and lungs ●

17. flow of blood between heart and rest of the body ●

a. systemic circulation

b. pulmonary circulation

CARDIOVASCULAR PROBLEMS

Circle the letter of the best answer for each question.

18. What's the best way to avoid heart problems?

a. 10 hours of sleep a night

b. a healthy diet and physical exercise

c. an easy life

d. a 10-mile run every day

Atherosclerosis

19. What is fat buildup in an artery called?

a. hypertension

b. heart attack

c. heart failure

d. atherosclerosis

20. What can cause a narrowing of the arteries?

a. hypertension

b. heart attack

c. heart failure

d. atherosclerosis

High Blood Pressure

21. What is another name for high blood pressure?

a. hypertension

b. heart attack

c. heart failure

d. atherosclerosis

Circle the letter of the best answer for each question.

22. What can happen when a brain artery clogs?

a. heart failure

b. heart attack

c. stroke

d. atherosclerosis

Heart Attacks and Heart Failure

23. What can happen when an artery that delivers blood to the heart become clogged?

a. hypertension

b. heart attack

c. heart failure

d. atherosclerosis

24. What cardiovascular problem happens when the heart cannot pump enough blood to meet the body's demands?

a. hypertension

b. heart attack

c. heart failure

d. atherosclerosis

Name ______________________________ Class ______________ Date ____________

Skills Worksheet

Directed Reading B

Section: Blood

Circle the letter of the best answer for each question.

1. How much blood does an adult have?

a. 5 liters

b. 10 liters

c. 50 liters

d. 100 liters

WHAT IS BLOOD?

2. What system is made of the heart, blood vessels, and blood?

a. skeletal system

b. muscular system

c. digestive system

d. circulatory system

3. What is blood made of?

a oxygen and plasma

b. red blood cells and white blood cells

c. plasma, red blood cells, platelets, and white blood cells

d. plasma and platelets

4. What does blood do?

a. carries oxygen and nutrients to your body

b. carries only oxygen to your body

c. carries carbon dioxide to your body

d. carries only nutrients to your body

Plasma

Circle the letter of the best answer for each question.

5. What is the plasma?

a. only white blood cells

b. only red blood cells

c. fluid part of blood

d. hemoglobin

Red Blood Cells

6. What makes up most blood cells?

a. red blood cells

b. white blood cells

c. platelets

d. plasma

7. Which cells receive oxygen from red blood cells?

a. all cells

b. only skin cells

c. only muscle cells

d. only bone cells

8. What attaches to the oxygen you breathe and carries oxygen on red blood cells?

a. plasma

b. hemoglobin

c. platelets

d. bone marrow

Platelets

Circle the letter of the best answer for each question.

9. Where are platelets made?

a. plasma

b. bone marrow

c. white blood cells

d. red blood cells

10. Why do platelets clump together?

a. to produce oxygen

b. to reduce oxygen

c. to produce blood loss

d. to reduce blood loss

White Blood Cells

11. What are pathogens?

a. disease-causing bacteria, other microorganisms, and viruses

b. large platelets

c. antibodies

d. tiny fibers

12. What destroys pathogens?

a. red blood cells

b. white blood cells

c. platelets

d. plasma

Circle the letter of the best answer for the question.

13. What part of the blood destroys dead and damaged cells?

a. white blood cells **c.** platelets

b. red blood cells **d.** pathogens

BODY TEMPERATURE REGULATION

Read the words in the box. Read the sentences. Fill in each blank with the word or phrase that best completes the sentence.

blood	temperature	blood vessels

14. Your ________________ helps regulate your body temperature.

15. When your body temperature rises, ________________ in your skin enlarge.

16. The transfer of heat from your blood to your skin helps lower your ________________.

BLOOD PRESSURE

diastolic	systolic	blood pressure

17. The force of blood pushing on walls of arteries is ________________.

18. The pressure inside large arteries when the ventricles contract is ________________ pressure.

19. The pressure inside arteries when the ventricles relax is ________________ pressure.

BLOOD TYPES

Read the words in the box. Read the sentences. Fill in each blank with the word or phrase that best completes the sentence.

antigens	antibodies	type A	type B

20. Chemicals on red blood cells that determine blood type are

______________________________.

21. Different blood types have different

______________________________ in the plasma.

22. Type A blood has ______________________________ antigens.

23. Type B blood has ______________________________ antigens.

BLOOD TYPES AND TRANSFUSIONS

Circle the letter of the best answer for each question.

24. What does a transfusion replace?

a. lost body temperature

b. lost pathogens

c. lost blood

d. lost antibodies

25. What could happen if you receive the wrong blood type?

a. Your blood type could change.

b. You might need more white blood cells.

c. You might get too much oxygen.

d. You could die.

Name ______________________ Class ______________ Date ______________

Skills Worksheet

Directed Reading B

Section: The Lymphatic System

Circle the letter of the best best answer for each question.

1. What group of organs and tissues collects excess fluids from cells?

a. lymphatic system

b. cardiovascular system

c. circulatory system

d. atria and ventricles

2. What does your lymphatic system help to fight?

a. antigens

b. antibodies

c. pathogens

d. lymph

VESSELS OF THE LYMPHATIC SYSTEM

Read the words in the box. Read the sentences. Fill in each blank with the word or phrase that best completes the sentence.

lymph	lymph capillaries	lymphatic vessels

3. The smallest lymph vessels are ______________________.

4. The lymphatic system collects a fluid called

______________________.

5. Lymph capillaries carry lymph into larger vessels called

______________________.

OTHER PARTS OF THE LYMPHATIC SYSTEM

Read the words in the box. Read the sentences. Fill in each blank with the word or phrase that best completes the sentence.

lymphocyte	bone marrow
killer T cell	lymph nodes

6. The soft tissue inside of bones, where blood cell are made, is called

______________________.

7. Small masses of tissue called ______________________ remove pathogens from lymph.

8. A type of white blood cell that fights pathogens is a

______________________.

9. Pathogens are destroyed by a kind of lymphocyte called a

______________________.

Thymus

Circle the letter of the best answer for each question.

10. What is the main gland of the lymphatic system?

a. spleen

b. tonsils

c. thymus

d. lymphocytes

11. What does the thymus make to fight infection?

a. spleen

b. tonsils

c. T cells

d. lymphocytes

Spleen

Circle the letter of the best answer for each question.

12. What is the largest lymphatic organ?

a. spleen

b. tonsils

c. lymph nodes

d. lymph

13. What does the spleen store and produce?

a. oxygen

b. blood

c. antigens

d. lymphocytes

14. What does the spleen's white pulp make?

a. new lymph

b. white blood cells that fight infection

c. antibodies

d. nodes

15. What does the spleen's red pulp remove from the blood?

a. fluids

b. damaged white blood cells

c. damaged red blood cells

d. oxygen

Tonsils

Circle the letter of the best answer for each question.

16. What is lymphatic tissue in the back of the mouth called?

a. spleen

b. tonsils

c. thymus

d. lymphocytes

17. What do tonsils fight?

a. bad breath

b. infection

c. antigens

d. antibodies

Name ______________________________ Class ________________ Date ______________

Skills Worksheet

Directed Reading B

Section: The Respiratory System

Circle the letter of the best answer for the question.

1. Why does the body need oxygen?

a. to get energy from food

b. to make its own food

c. to fight infection

d. to make more blood

RESPIRATION AND THE CIRCULATORY SYSTEM

Read the description. Then, draw a line from the dot next to each description to the matching word.

2. the process of using oxygen and releasing carbon dioxide and water ●

3. the process of inhaling and exhaling ●

4. the organs that take in oxygen and get rid of carbon dioxide ●

a. respiration

b. respiratory system

c. breathing

---

5. the main passage of the respiratory system ●

6. the part of the throat that produces sounds ●

7. the throat ●

a. pharynx

b. nose

c. larynx

Trachea

Circle the letter of the best answer for each question.

8. What is the trachea also called?

a. nose

b. throat

c. tonsils

d. windpipe

9. What goes through the trachea?

a. blood to the heart

b. air to the lungs

c. food to the stomach

d. lymph to the lymph nodes

Bronchi and Alveoli

10. What is a tube connecting the lungs with the trachea?

a. pharynx

b. nose

c. larynx

d. bronchus

11. What are bronchioles?

a. smaller branches of bronchi

b. tiny sacs in the lungs

c. tubes next to the larynx

d. pharynx

12. What are alveoli?

a. smaller branches of bronchi

b. tiny air sacs in the lungs

c. tubes next to the larynx

d. pharynx

BREATHING

Read the words in the box. Read the sentences. Fill in each blank with the word or phrase that best completes the sentence.

diaphragm	muscles

13. When you inhale, the ______________________ contracts.

14. When the diaphragm contracts, the rib ______________________ contract and lift the rib cage.

BREATHING AND CELLULAR RESPIRATION

oxygen	energy

15. When you breathe, you take in ______________________.

16. Cells use oxygen to release ______________________.

RESPIRATORY DISORDERS

Circle the letter of the best answer for each question.

17. What may trigger asthma?

a. blood cells

b. dust or pollen

c. antigens

d. SARS

18. What causes SARS?

a. blood cells

b. dust or pollen

c. virus

d. bacteria

Name ______________________ Class ______________ Date ______________

Assessment

Chapter Test C

Circulation and Respiration

MULTIPLE CHOICE

Circle the letter of the best answer for each question.

1. What system includes the heart and blood vessels?

a. digestive system

b. lymphatic system

c. cardiovascular system

d. respiratory system

2. What does the heart do?

a. pumps blood

b. fights disease

c. exchanges gases

d. carries blood

3. What do blood vessels do?

a. pump blood

b. fight disease

c. exchange gases

d. carry blood

4. What are the two types of circulation?

a. systolic and diastolic

b. pulmonary and systemic

c. RBC and WBC

d. plasma and platelet

MULTIPLE CHOICE

Circle the letter of the best answer for each question.

5. Heart attacks and hypertension are problems of which body system?

a. cardiovascular

b. respiratory

c. lymphatic

d. digestive

6. What are alveoli?

a. tubes that connect the throat and lungs

b. tiny air sacs in the lungs

c. the vocal cords in the throat

d. the passage from the mouth to the larynx

7. What is the trachea?

a. a tube that connects the throat and lungs

b. the vocal cords in the throat

c. a tiny air sacs in the lungs

d. the passage from the mouth to the larynx

8. What is the pharynx?

a. a tube that connects the throat and lungs

b. the vocal cords in the throat

c. a tiny air sacs in the lungs

d. the passage from the mouth to the larynx

MATCHING

Read the description. Then, draw a line from the dot next to each description to the matching word.

9. plasma, red blood cells, white blood cells, and platelets ●
10. arteries, veins, and capillaries ●
11. force of blood when the heart beats ●
12. A, B, AB, and O ●

a. blood types
b. blood pressure
c. blood vessels
d. blood components

---

13. upper chamber of heart ●
14. sound made by valves ●
15. lower chamber of heart ●
16. structure that stops blood from flowing backward ●

a. atrium
b. ventricle
c. valve
d. heartbeat

FILL-IN-THE-BLANK

Read the words in the box. Read the sentences. <u>Fill in each blank</u> with the word or phrase that best completes the sentence.

lymph	capillary	lymph nodes

17. The smallest lymph vessel is a lymph

______________________.

18. Extra fluid collected by the lymphatic system is called ______________________.

19. Pathogens can be removed from the lymph by

______________________.

spleen	thymus	tonsils

20. Killer T cells are made in the ______________________.

21. The largest lymphatic gland in the body is the ______________________.

22. The lymphatic tissues in the back of the mouth are the

______________________.

Name ______________________ Class ______________ Date ____________

Skills Worksheet

Directed Reading B

Section: The Digestive System

Circle the letter of the best answer for each question.

1. What is the digestive system?

a. the liver, pancreas, and small intestine

b. a group of organs that work together to digest food

c. the large intestine, gall bladder, and esophagus

d. a group of veins and arteries that work together to digest food

DIGESTIVE SYSTEM AT A GLANCE

2. Which of the following is NOT part of the digestive tract?

a. stomach

b. esophagus

c. kidneys

d. large intestine

3. Food does NOT pass through which of these organs?

a. stomach

b. pharynx

c. small intestine

d. liver

BREAKING DOWN FOOD

4. What are the two kinds of digestion?

a. mechanical and chemical

b. mechanical and liquid

c. mechanical and solid

d. mechanical and heat

Read the words in the box. Read the sentences. Fill in each blank with the word or phrase that best completes the sentence.

chemical	amino acids	mechanical
enzymes		

5. Chewing your food is ______________________ digestion.

6. When your body breaks food down into nutrients, it is ______________________ digestion.

7. Proteins are made up of chains of ______________________.

8. The substances called ______________________ cut up the protein chains.

DIGESTION BEGINS IN THE MOUTH

Circle the letter of the best answer for each question.

9. How does chewing help digestion?

a. chewing makes food taste better.

b. chewing makes food last longer.

c. chewing makes food smaller.

d. chewing makes it harder for bacteria to grow.

Teeth

Read the description. Then, draw a line from the dot next to each description to the matching word.

10. These teeth are used for mashing food. •

11. These teeth are used for grinding food. •

12. These teeth are used for shredding food. •

a. premolars

b. incisors and canines

c. molars

Saliva

Read the words in the box. Read the sentences. Fill in each blank with the word or phrase that best completes the sentence.

esophagus	tongue	saliva

13. As you chew your food, it is mixed with

______________________.

14. When your food is soft, the ______________________ pushes it from your mouth to your throat.

15. The tube that squeezes the food into your stomach is called the ______________________.

THE HARSH ENVIRONMENT OF THE STOMACH

chyme	enzymes	stomach
small intestine		

16. The muscular contractions of the ______________________ squeeze the food.

17. Acid and ______________________ in the stomach break food into nutrients.

18. When the food moves out of the stomach, it is a soupy mixture called ______________________.

19. When the chyme leaves the stomach, it goes to the ______________________.

THE PANCREAS AND SMALL INTESTINE

The Pancreas

Circle the letter of the best answer for each question.

20. The pancreas makes fluid. What organ does the fluid protect?

a. the stomach

b. the small intestine

c. the esophagus

d. the tongue

21. The pancreas produces hormones. What do the hormones do?

a. regulate blood sugar

b. regulate bile

c. regulate carbohydrates

d. regulate proteins

The Small Intestine

22. What do the villi in the small intestine do?

a. kill bacteria

b. protect the small intestine

c. absorb nutrients

d. protect the blood

23. Why is the small intestine called "small"?

a. It is short.

b. It is small in diameter.

c. It doesn't hold much.

d. It doesn't weigh much.

THE LIVER AND GALLBLADDER

Circle the letter of the best answer for each question.

24. Which of the following is NOT the job of the liver?

a. breaking up proteins

b. storing nutrients

c. breaking down toxins

d. breaking up fat

Breaking up Fat

25. Which of the following IS the job of the gallbladder?

a. storing bile

b. storing nutrients

c. breaking down toxins

d. breaking up proteins

26. What does bile do to large fat droplets?

a. It turns them into nutrients.

b. It changes them to water.

c. It breaks them into tiny droplets.

d. It changes them to enzymes.

Storing Nutrients and Protecting the Body

Read the words in the box. Read the sentences. Fill in each blank with the word or phrase that best completes the sentence.

liver	bloodstream	chemicals

27. After nutrients are broken down, they are absorbed into the ______________________________.

28. Nutrients that the body doesn't need right away are stored by the ______________________________.

29. The liver helps protect the body by making many ______________________________ harmless.

THE END OF THE LINE

Circle the letter of the best answer for each question.

30. What happens to material that can't be absorbed into the blood?

a. It goes back to the stomach.

b. It is pushed into the large intestine.

c. It is broken down by the liver.

d. It goes to the small intestine.

In the Large Intestine

31. Which of the following is NOT the job of the large intestine?

a. absorbing water

b. producing feces

c. producing fiber

d. storing extra material

Leaving the Body

Read the words in the box. Read the sentences. Fill in each blank with the word or phrase that best completes the sentence.

rectum	anus	fiber

32. Another name for a carbohydrate called cellulose is ______________________.

33. Solid waste, or feces is stored in the ______________________ until it can leave the body.

34. Solid waste leaves the body by being expelled through the ______________________.

Name ______________________ Class ______________ Date ____________

Skills Worksheet

Directed Reading B

Section: The Urinary System

Circle the letter of the best answer for each question.

1. What is excretion?

a. digesting food

b. breathing

c. removing waste from the body

d. adding nutrients to the body

CLEANING THE BLOOD

2. Which two waste products does the urinary system remove from the blood?

a. urine and sweat

b. fluids and blood

c. carbon dioxide and ammonia

d. carbon monoxide and ammonia

THE KIDNEYS AS FILTERS

Read the words in the box. Read the sentences. Fill in each blank with the word or phrase that best completes the sentence.

nephrons	kidneys	urea

3. Your blood is constantly cleansed by a pair of organs called ______________________.

4. The microscopic filters called ______________________ remove wastes from the blood.

5. One harmful substance removed by the nephrons is ______________________.

WATER IN, WATER OUT

Sweat and Thirst

Circle the letter of the best answer for each question.

6. Why do humans sweat?

a. to clean the skin

b. to cool the body

c. to make saliva

d. to get rid of thirst

Antidiuretic Hormone

7. What does an antidiuretic hormone (ADH) cause the kidneys to do?

a. make more urine

b. make no urine

c. make the same amount of urine

d. make less urine

Diuretics

8. Which of the following causes the kidneys to make more urine?

a. a diuretic

b. blood

c. an ADH

d. sweat

URINARY SYSTEM PROBLEMS

9. What are kidney stones made of?

a. viruses

b. waste materials

c. ADH

d. bacteria

Circle the letter of the best answer for each question.

10. How can bacteria get into the bladder?

a. through the ureter

b. through the urine

c. through the urethra

d. through the urea

11. What might happen if nephrons are damaged?

a. Kidneys can become diseased.

b. Kidney stones can form.

c. Bacteria can enter the kidneys.

d. Kidneys will make more urine.

Name ________________________ Class ______________ Date ____________

Assessment

Chapter Test C

The Digestive and Urinary System

MULTIPLE CHOICE

Circle the letter of the best answer for each question.

1. What are the two kinds of digestion?

a. mechanical and chemical

b. liquid and solid

c. digestive and urinary

d. food and drink

2. How is chewing helpful for digestion?

a. Chewing makes food last longer.

b. Chewing makes food taste better.

c. Chewing makes food smaller.

d. Chewing helps viruses grow.

3. How does your stomach squeeze the food in it?

a. with stomach acid

b. with digestion

c. with muscular contractions

d. with chyme

4. What organ does the pancreas protect with fluid?

a. the stomach

b. the small intestine

c. the large intestine

d. the esophagus

MULTIPLE CHOICE

Circle the letter of the best answer for each question.

5. What takes in nutrients in the small intestine?

a. chyme
b. enzymes
c. villi
d. urethra

6. After nutrients are broken down, where do they go?

a. to the brain
b. to the pancreas
c. to the stomach
d. to the bloodstream

7. What is excretion?

a. removing waste from the body
b. digesting food
c. breathing
d. adding nutrients

8. What do the kidneys do?

a. digest food
b. absorb nutrients
c. indicate hunger
d. clean the blood

9. What does the liver store?

a. urine
b. toxins
c. nutrients
d. bile

10. What does the gallbladder store?

a. fat
b. toxins
c. nutrients
d. bile

MATCHING

Read the description. Then, draw a line from the dot next to each description to the matching word.

11. the tube that squeezes food into the stomach ●
12. the organ where nutrients are absorbed ●
13. the organ that breaks down toxins ●
14. the organ that changes food into chyme ●

a. small intestine
b. esophagus
c. stomach
d. liver

---

15. can block urine flow ●
16. filters blood in the kidneys ●
17. tells the kidneys to make less urine ●
18. can cause infection in the urinary system ●

a. bacteria
b. nephrons
c. antidiuretic hormones
d. kidney stones

FILL-IN-THE-BLANK

Read the words in the box. Read the sentences. Fill in each blank with the word or phrase that best completes the sentence.

digestive system	large intestine	liver
premolars	incisors	urinary system

19. The group of organs working together so your body can use food is the ________________.

20. The group of organs working together so your body can get rid of wastes is the ________________.

21. Teeth that mash food are called ________________.

22. Teeth that shred food are called ________________.

23. The organ that makes bile to break down fat is the ________________.

24. The organ that changes liquid waste into feces is called the ________________.

Name ______________________ Class ______________ Date ____________

Skills Worksheet

Directed Reading B

Section: The Nervous System

TWO SYSTEMS WITHIN A SYSTEM

Circle the letter of the best answer for each question.

1. What does the nervous system do?

a. pump blood

b. gather and interpret information

c. digest food

d. eliminate waste

Read the words in the box. Read the sentences. Fill in each blank with the word or phrase that best completes the sentence.

central	information	responds
peripheral	central command post	

2. The nervous system is the body's ______________________.

3. The nervous system gathers and interprets ______________________.

4. The nervous system ______________________ to information as needed.

5. Your brain and spinal cord are the ______________________ nervous system.

6. The ______________________ nervous system does NOT include the brain and spinal cord.

THE PERIPHERAL NERVOUS SYSTEM

<u>Circle the letter</u> of the best answer for each question.

7. What are special cells in your body that transfer messages called?

a. impulses
b. homeostasis
c. neurons
d. cell bodies

8. What are fast-moving electrical messages that travel along nerve cells called?

a. impulses
b. dendrites
c. axons
d. cell bodies

Neuron Structure

Read the description. Then, <u>draw a line</u> from the dot next to each description to the matching word.

9. allows the neuron to receive information ●

10. carry impulses from the cell body ●

11. has a nucleus and cell organelles ●

a. cell body
b. dendrite
c. axon

Information Collection

<u>Circle the letter</u> of the best answer for each question.

12. Which neurons gather information about what is happening in your body?

a. motor neurons
b. sensory neurons
c. receptors
d. light

Circle the letter of the best answer for each question.

13. What are the specialized nerve endings at the end of the sensory neurons?

a. motor neurons

b. sensory neurons

c. receptors

d. light

Delivering Orders

14. What neurons send impulses from the brain and spinal cord?

a. motor neurons

b. sensory neurons

c. receptors

d. light

15. What connects the central nervous system to the rest of the body?

a. axons

b. nerves

c. blood vessels

d. connective tissue

16. Where are all of the nerves in your body?

a. in your head

b. in your spine

c. in your muscles

d. everywhere

NERVES

17. Which of these are a part of nerves?

a. skeletal muscle

b. skin

c. axons

d. homeostasis

SOMATIC AND AUTONOMIC NERVOUS SYSTEMS

Read the words in the box. Read the sentences. Fill in each blank with the word or phrase that best completes the sentence.

voluntary	somatic
autonomic	homeostasis

18. Most of the ______________________ nervous system is under your conscious control.

19. The somatic nervous system controls ______________________ movements, such as smiling.

20. Digestion and heart rate are functions controlled by the ______________________ nervous system.

21. The sympathetic and parasympathetic nervous systems work together for ______________________.

THE CENTRAL NERVOUS SYSTEM

The Control Center

voluntary	involuntary	brain

22. The main control center of the central nervous system is the ______________________.

23. Things the brain controls that happen without thinking are called ______________________.

24. When you move your arm, the action is ______________________.

The Cerebrum

Circle the letter of the best answer for the question.

25. What is the largest part of your brain?

a. right hemisphere

b. top of brain

c. cerebrum

d. medulla

Read the words in the box. Read the sentences. Fill in each blank with the word or phrase that best completes the sentence.

hemisphere	cerebrum

26. You think and store memories in the

______________________________.

27. Your right hand is controlled by the left

______________________________ of the cerebrum.

The Cerebellum

Circle the letter of the best answer for each question.

28. What part of your brain helps you keep your balance?

a. cerebrum

b. hemisphere

c. cerebellum

d. medulla

The Medulla

Circle the letter of the best answer for each question.

29. What is one involuntary process the medulla controls?

a. balance

b. talking

c. memory

d. heart rate

THE SPINAL CORD

30. The bones that protect your spinal cord are called

a. neurons.

b. homeostasis.

c. vertices.

d. vertebrae.

Spinal Cord Injury

31. What is one good way to avoid spinal cord injuries?

a. don't play sports

b. don't drive a car

c. wear a seat belt

d. exercise a lot

Name ______________________ Class ______________ Date ____________

Skills Worksheet

Directed Reading B

Section: Responding to the Environment

Circle the letter of the best answer for each question.

1. What do you call awareness caused when sensory messages reach the brain?

a. receptors

b. recognition

c. sensation

d. heartbeat

SENSE OF TOUCH

2. What type of receptor feels temperature?

a. thermoreceptor

b. vibration receptor

c. sound receptor

d. pressure receptor

3. Which of these is NOT sensed by skin receptors?

a. vibration

b. pressure

c. pain

d. light

4. What system protects the body from damage?

a. nervous system

b. receptor system

c. sensory system

d. integumentary system

RESPONDING TO SENSORY MESSAGES

Circle the letter of the best answer for the question.

5. What is a very fast, involuntary action called?

a. pain

b. sensation

c. reflex

d. stimulus

Feedback Mechanisms

Read the words in the box. Read the sentences. Fill in each blank with the word or phrase that best completes the sentence.

feedback mechanism	receptors	brain

6. The brain processes information from skin ______________________.

7. Receptors send impulses to the ______________________.

8. Your body's cooling process is a ______________________.

SENSE OF SIGHT

Circle the letter of the best answer for the question.

9. What is the light-sensitive, inner layer of the eye called?

a. retina

b. pupil

c. cornea

d. photoreceptor

Draw a line from each term to the matching number on the picture.

iris lens optic nerve retina

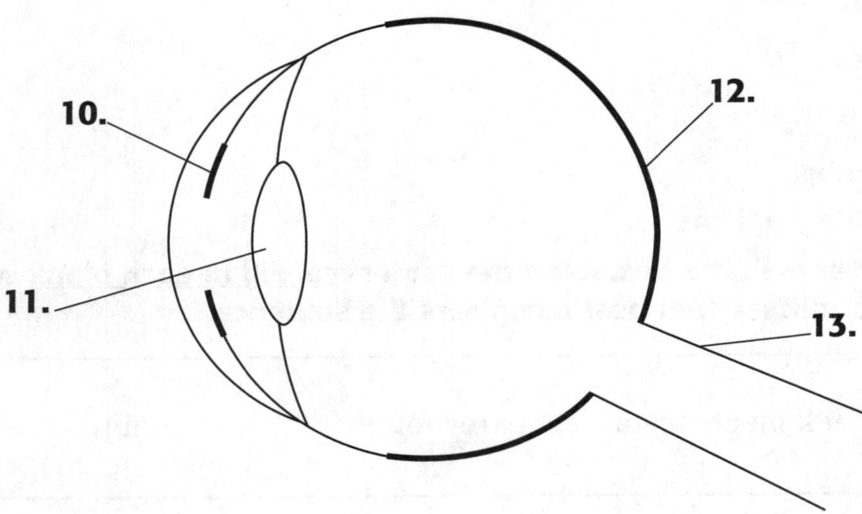

Reacting to Light

Circle the letter of the best answer for each question.

14. What opening lets light into the eye?

a. pupil

c. retina

b. iris

d. rods

15. What controls the light going into the eye?

a. pupil

c. retina

b. iris

d. rods

Focusing the Light

<u>Circle the letter</u> of the best answer for each question.

16. What is the clear, curved material behind the pupil?

a. pupil

b. lens

c. retina

d. rods

17. What happens when the lens focuses light in front of the retina?

a. nearsightedness

b. farsightedness

c. blindness

d. normal vision

18. What happens when the lens focuses light behind the retina?

a. nearsightedness

b. farsightedness

c. blindness

d. normal vision

SENSE OF HEARING

Read the description. Then, <u>draw a line</u> from the dot next to each description to the matching word.

19. tube in the inner ear you must have to hear	●	**a.** eardrum
20. funnels sound to middle ear	●	**b.** outer ear
21. thin membrane between middle and outer ear	●	**c.** cochlea

SENSE OF TASTE

Circle the letter of the best answer for each question.

22. The four kinds of taste buds are salty, sweet, sour, and

a. bitter.

c. rancid.

b. acid.

d. peppery.

Read the description. Then, draw a line from the dot next to each description to the matching word.

23. tiny bumps covering the tongue ●	**a.** taste buds
24. inside papillae ●	**b.** papillae
25. inside taste buds ●	**c.** taste cells

SENSE OF SMELL

Read the words in the box. Read the sentences. Fill in each blank with the word or phrase that best completes the sentence.

taste	olfactory	molecules

26. The nasal cavity is lined with ______________________ cells.

27. Smell and ______________________ are closely related.

28. You smell something when ______________________ are inhaled.

Name ______________________ Class ______________ Date ______________

Skills Worksheet

Directed Reading B

Section: The Endocrine System

Circle the letter of the best answer for each question.

1. Which of the following processes is controlled by your endocrine system?

a. vision

b. growth

c. reflex action

d. speech

HORMONES AS CHEMICAL MESSENGERS

Read the words in the box. Read the sentences. Fill in each blank with the word or phrase that best completes the sentence.

bloodstream	gland	endocrine
hormones	epinephrine	

2. Body functions are controlled by the

______________________ system.

3. A group of cells that makes chemicals for the body

is a(n) ______________________.

4. Chemicals made by the endocrine glands are

called ______________________.

5. Hormones flow to the whole body through

the ______________________.

6. The hormone that produces the "fight or flight"

response is ______________________.

MORE ENDOCRINE GLANDS

Circle the letter of the best answer for each question.

7. What is a chemical messenger that causes changes in the body?

a. gland

b. hormone

c. blood

d. endocrine system

8. What cells does the thymus gland grow that destroy invading cells?

a. killer T cells

b. hormone cells

c. pituitary cells

d. epinephrine cells

Read the description. Then, draw a line from the dot next to each description to the matching word.

9. speeds up use of energy ●

10. produces hormones needed by males to reproduce ●

11. produces hormones needed by females to reproduce ●

12. help the body respond to danger ●

a. thyroid gland

b. adrenal gland

c. testes

d. ovaries

CONTROLLING THE ENDOCRINE GLANDS

Read the words in the box. Read the sentences. Fill in each blank with the word or phrase that best completes the sentence.

glands	feedback	hormones

13. Endocrine glands are controlled by ______________________ mechanisms.

14. Feedback mechanisms tell ______________________ to stop making hormones.

15. Chemical messages tell endocrine glands to start or stop making certain ______________________.

Read the description. Then draw a line from the dot next to each description to the matching word.

16. endocrine gland makes the wrong amount of a hormone •

17. pancreas doesn't make enough insulin •

18. person with diabetes needs daily injections •

19. levels regulated by insulin •

a. insulin

b. hormone imbalance

c. diabetes

d. blood-glucose

---

20. pituitary gland doesn't make enough growth hormone •

21. possible treatment prescribed for stunted growth •

22. pituitary gland makes too much growth hormone •

a. growth hormone

b. child is too tall

c. child is too short

Name ______________________ Class ______________ Date ____________

Assessment

Chapter Test C

Communication and Control

MULTIPLE CHOICE

Circle the letter of the best answer for each question.

1. Which part of the brain is used for thinking and memory?

a. medulla

b. cerebrum

c. cerebellum

d. thymus

2. What connects your body to the central nervous system?

a. neurons

b. nerves

c. brain

d. muscle

3. What body system does skin belong to?

a. nervous

b. spinal

c. integumentary

d. solar

4. A group of cells that make special chemicals in your body is called a

a. cerebellum

b. receptor

c. gland

d. cerebrum

MATCHING

Read the description. Then, draw a line from the dot next to each description to the matching word.

5. includes the spinal cord and brain ●

6. controls body functions you don't think about ●

7. carries nerve impulses to muscles or glands ●

8. gathers information from inside or around the body ●

a. central nervous system

b. autonomic nervous system

c. sensory neuron

d. motor neuron

---

9. helps the body respond to danger ●

10. releases hormones that affect other glands and organs ●

11. increases the rate you use energy ●

12. regulates the immune system ●

a. thymus

b. adrenal gland

c. thyroid gland

d. pituitary gland

FILL-IN-THE-BLANK

Read the words in the box. Read the sentences. Fill in each blank with the word or phrase that best completes the sentence.

involuntary	axons	diabetes
pancreas	cochlea	papillae

13. Long nerve fibers that carry impulses to other cells

are ______________________.

14. The medulla controls ______________________ processes.

15. Blood-glucose levels in your body are controlled by

the ______________________.

16. A person whose body cannot make enough insulin

has ______________________.

17. The tube in the inner ear necessary for hearing is

the ______________________.

18. The tiny bumps that cover the tongue

are ______________________.

MATCHING

Draw a line from each term to the matching number on the picture.

retina pupil optic nerve iris

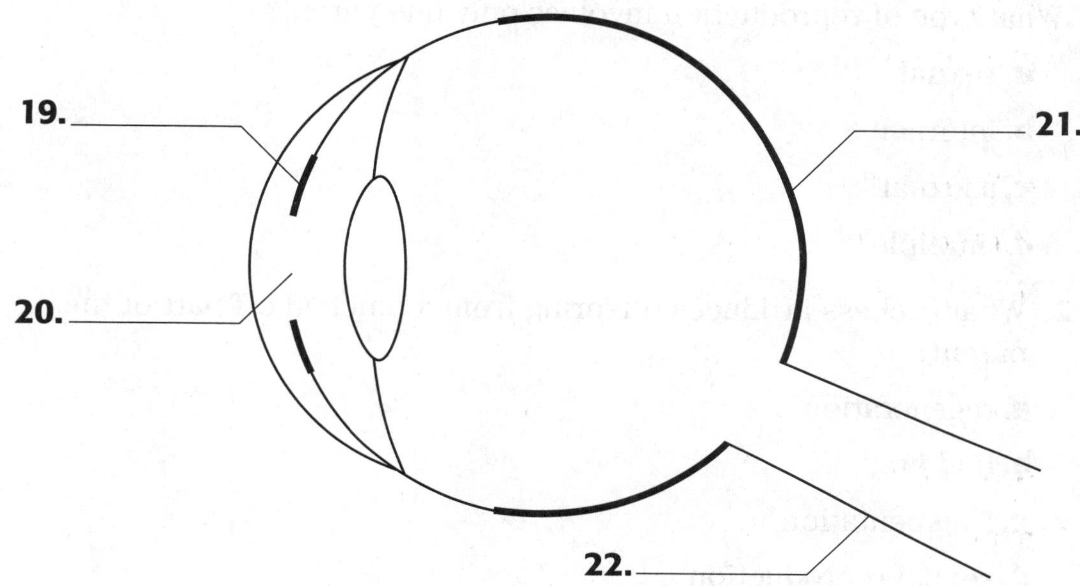

Name ______________________ Class ______________ Date ____________

Skills Worksheet

Directed Reading B

Section: Animal Reproduction

ASEXUAL REPRODUCTION

Circle the letter of the best answer for each question.

1. What type of reproduction involves only one parent?

a. sexual

b. internal

c. asexual

d. multiple

2. What process produces offspring from a pinched off part of the parent?

a. regeneration

b. budding

c. fragmentation

d. sexual reproduction

3. Fragmentation occurs when a broken-off part of an animal grows into what?

a. a new limb

b. a segment

c. a new individual

d. a sex cell

4. When an animal loses a body part that grows into a new organism, it is called what?

a. sexual reproduction

b. regeneration

c. budding

d. separation

SEXUAL REPRODUCTION

Circle the letter of the best answer for each question.

5. In sexual reproduction, what cells unite to create offspring?

a. genes

b. chromosomes

c. two parents

d. sex cells

6. What is the female sex cell called?

a. an egg

b. a zygote

c. a sperm

d. a chromosome

7. Sexual reproduction forms an offspring that gets what from its two parents?

a. genetic information

b. zygotes

c. meiosis

d. fertilized

8. A female's egg is fertilized when it joins with what?

a. chromosomes

b. meiosis

c. male's sperm

d. zygotes

INTERNAL AND EXTERNAL FERTILIZATION

Circle the letter of the best answer for each question.

9. In external fertilization, where are the female's eggs fertilized?

a. under water

b. inside her body

c. on the land

d. outside her body

Internal Fertilization

10. In internal fertilization, where do the sex cells unite?

a. in the male's body

b. in the female's body

c. in the egg

d. in the sperm

11. What is one good thing about internal fertilization?

a. Sperm are deposited over the egg mass.

b. Offspring develop quickly.

c. Eggs are protected inside mothers.

d. Many eggs are fertilized together.

MAMMALS

12. Where does a marsupial offspring develop after it is born?

a. in the mother's pouch

b. in its shell

c. in the father's body

d. in the mother's belly

Circle the letter of the best answer for each question.

13. What are animals whose offspring develop inside their mother's body?

a. monotremes

b. placental mammals

c. kangaroos

d. marsupials

14. A monotreme is a mammal that does what?

a. uses external fertilization

b. gives birth to live young

c. lays eggs

d. feeds young with a placenta

Name ______________________ Class ______________ Date ____________

Skills Worksheet

Directed Reading B

Section: Human Reproduction

THE MALE REPRODUCTIVE SYSTEM

Read the description. Then, draw a line from the dot to the matching word.

1. This makes semen. ●

2. This makes sperm and testosterone. ●

3. Semen travels through this tube. ●

4. This outside organ puts semen into a female. ●

a. urethra

b. testis

c. penis

d. prostate gland

---

5. male sex hormone ●

6. place where sperm are stored ●

7. tube that leads to the prostate gland ●

8. mixture of sperm and fluid ●

a. vas deferens

b. semen

c. testosterone

d. epididymis

THE FEMALE REPRODUCTIVE SYSTEM

The Egg's Journey

9. place where eggs are usually fertilized ●

10. time when eggs are released ●

11. place where a fertilized egg develops ●

12. passage through which babies come out during birth ●

a. the uterus

b. the fallopian tube

c. the vagina

d. during ovulation

Circle the letter of the best answer for each question.

13. What are the female organs that make eggs?

a. the fallopian tubes

b. the uterus

c. the ovaries

d. the vagina

14. Which one of the following are female sex hormones?

a. testosterone and estrogen

b. chromosome and testosterone

c. estrogen and progesterone

d. ovulation and estrogen

Menstrual Cycle

Read the description. Then draw a line from the dot next to each description to the matching word.

15. uterus sheds blood and tissue ●	**a.** a complete menstrual cycle
16. 14th day of the cycle ●	**b.** first day of menstruation
17. about 28 days ●	**c.** ovulation happens

MULTIPLE BIRTHS

Read the words in the box. Read the sentences. Fill in each blank with the word or phrase that best completes the sentence.

multiple birth	identical twins	fraternal twins

18. Having more than one baby at the same time is called a(n)

______________________________.

19. Twins that do not look alike are called

______________________________.

20. Twins that have the same genes and look exactly alike are called

______________________________.

REPRODUCTIVE SYSTEM PROBLEMS

STDs

Circle the letter of the best answer for each question.

21. How does a person get a sexually transmitted disease?

a. from coughing

b. from sexual contact

c. from dirty bathrooms

d. from shaking hands

22. Which one of the following is an STD, or sexually transmitted disease?

a. AIDS

b. the flu

c. a cold

d. cancer

Cancer

Circle the letter of the best answer for each question.

23. Cancer is caused by the uncontrolled growth of what?

a. eggs

b. zygotes

c. body cells

d. the uterus

24. What is a common reproductive cancer of men?

a. prostate cancer

b. penis cancer

c. liver cancer

d. cervix cancer

25. What is a common reproductive cancer of women?

a. prostate cancer

b. penis cancer

c. liver cancer

d. cancer of the cervix

Infertility

26. Infertile couples cannot do what?

a. produce sperm

b. get STDs

c. have children

d. get cancer

27. What is one cause of infertility in men?

a. liver disease

b. too few offspring

c. abnormal ovulation

d. few healthy sperm

Name ______________________ Class ______________ Date ____________

Skills Worksheet

Directed Reading B

Section: Growth and Development

FROM FERTILIZATION TO EMBRYO

Circle the letter of the best answer for each question.

1. Where does the sperm usually fertilize the egg?

a. in the uterus

b. in a fallopian tube

c. in a membrane

d. in a nucleus

2. What is an embryo?

a. a newborn baby

b. one fertilized egg

c. a ball of cells

d. a million sperm

3. What is it called when the zygote attaches itself to the uterus?

a. fertilization

b. implantation

c. multiple birth

d. menstrual cycle

FROM EMBRYO TO FETUS

4. Through what organ does the mother nourish the developing embryo?

a. the uterus

b. the placenta

c. the fallopian tube

d. the cervix

Weeks 1 to 4

<u>Circle the letter</u> of the best answer for each question.

5. Which of the following begins during the first 4 weeks of pregnancy?

a. The embryo grows fingernails.

b. The embryo can kick its feet.

c. The embryo can see light.

d. The embryo has a heartbeat.

Weeks 5 to 8

6. What connects the embryo to the placenta?

a. the amnion

b. the umbilical cord

c. the fallopian tube

d. the spinal cord

7. During weeks 5 to 8, what part of the embryo grows quickly?

a. its arms

b. its muscles

c. its brain

d. its taste buds

Weeks 9 to 16

8. What is the unborn child called after 8 weeks of development?

a. a fetus

b. an embryo

c. an infant

d. a zygote

Circle the letter of the best answer for each question.

9. Which of the following does NOT happen to the fetus during weeks 9 to 16?

a. It doubles in size.

b. Its muscles grow stronger.

c. It can hear sounds.

d. It makes movements the mother can feel.

Weeks 17 to 24

10. By week 17, what can the fetus respond to?

a. heat

b. language

c. sound

d. colors

Weeks 25 to 36

11. By week 32, light may affect the way the fetus does what?

a. moves

b. sleeps

c. breathes

d. eats

BIRTH

12. What are the contractions a mother feels when giving birth?

a. full-term

b. placenta

c. labor

d. uterus

Circle the letter of the best answer for each question.

13. A baby comes out of what part of a mother's body?

a. her vagina

b. her placenta

c. her uterus

d. her cervix

FROM BIRTH TO DEATH

Infancy and Childhood

14. A child is called an infant until it reaches what age?

a. 1 year old

b. 2 years old

c. 3 years old

d. 5 years old

15. What is one change you experience during childhood?

a. you get baby teeth

b. you grow hair

c. you learn how to walk

d. you get permanent teeth

Adolescence

16. What happens during puberty?

a. You get permanent teeth.

b. Your nervous system develops.

c. Your reproductive system matures.

d. Your muscles become coordinated.

Adulthood

Circle the letter of the best answer for each question.

17. What reaches its peak when you are a young adult?

a. your aging process

b. your physical development

c. your body fat

d. your wealth

18. What is a common sign of aging in older adults?

a. greater flexibility

b. blindness

c. graying of hair

d. inability to walk

Name ______________________ Class ______________ Date ____________

Assessment

Chapter Test C

MULTIPLE CHOICE

Circle the letter of the best answer for each question.

1. Which one of the following is a form of asexual reproduction?

a. fertilization
b. meiosis
c. budding
d. twinning

2. What cells unite in sexual reproduction?

a. embryo cells
b. sperm and fluid
c. sperm and egg
d. budding cells

3. What type of reproduction involves a female's eggs being fertilized outside her body?

a. internal
b. external
c. moist
d. sperm

4. Eggs are protected in the mother's body with what type of fertilization?

a. regeneration
b. zygote
c. internal
d. external

5. What do we call an animal whose young develops in a pouch?

a. marsupial
b. budding
c. mammal
d. placenta

6. Which male organ produces sperm?

a. the penis
b. the urethra
c. the ovary
d. the testis

Circle the letter of the words that best answer the questions.

7. Which female organ produces eggs?

a. the vagina

b. the uterus

c. the bladder

d. the ovary

8. A fertilized egg develops in which female organ?

a. the uterus

b. the fallopian tube

c. the vagina

d. the ovulation

9. What is the 28-day period that prepares a female's body for pregnancy?

a. puberty

b. labor

c. ovulation cycle

d. menstrual cycle

10. Two babies born together that look exactly alike are called what?

a. fraternal twins

b. identical twins

c. quintuplets

d. quadruplets

11. What is one sexually transmitted disease a person can get during sex?

a. the flu

b. zygote

c. pneumonia

d. chlamydia

Circle the letter of the words that best answer the questions.

12. When cells grow in an uncontrolled way, what may develop?

a. an embryo

b. a cancer

c. a zygote

d. hepatitis

13. Couples who cannot have children are said to be what?

a. infertile

b. in labor

c. asexual

d. ovulating

MATCHING

Read the description. Then, draw a line from the dot to the matching word.

14. an unborn baby when it is just a ball of cells ●

15. an unborn baby after 9 or 10 weeks of pregnancy ●

16. this connects the unborn baby to its mother's placenta ●

a. umbilical cord

b. fetus

c. embryo

---

17. this grows quickly during weeks 7 to 8 of pregnancy ●

18. a 19-week-old fetus can respond to this ●

19. a mother's contractions as a baby is born ●

a. brain

b. labor

c. sound

FILL-IN-THE-BLANK

Read the words in the box. Read the sentences. <u>Fill in each blank</u> with the word or phrase that best completes the sentence.

infant	childhood
adolescence	young adulthood

20. During ______________________________, a person's reproductive system matures.

21. A child is called a(n) ______________________________ until it is 2 years old.

22. When people are in ______________________________, they are at the peak of their physical development.

23. During ______________________________, you grow a set of permanent teeth.

Name ______________________ Class ______________ Date ____________

Skills Worksheet

Directed Reading B

Section: Disease

CAUSES OF DISEASE

Circle the letter of the best answer for each question.

1. What kind of disease does not spread from person to person?

a. noninfectious

b. infectious

c. streptococcus

d. pathogen

2. What might cause a noninfectious disease?

a. dirty hands

b. a genetic disorder

c. being around sick people

d. being sneezed on

3. Which one of these might cause a noninfectious disease?

a. sharing straws

b. working in a hospital

c. getting an infection

d. eating too much fat

4. What kind of disease is spread from person to person?

a. noninfectious

b. infectious

c. streptococcus

d. pathogen

5. What causes infectious diseases?

a. genetic disorder

b. heredity

c. pathogens

d. smoking

Circle the letter of the best answer for each question.

6. What are two examples of pathogens?

a. poor diet and no exercise

b. smoking and heredity

c. bleeding and heart problems

d. viruses and worms

PATHWAYS TO PATHOGENS

Read the description. Then, draw a line from the dot next to each description to the matching word.

7. sends pathogens through air	●	**a.** doorknob
8. might have pathogens left on it	●	**b.** sneeze
9. spreads pathogens in a friendly way	●	**c.** Lyme disease
10. a disease spread by ticks	●	**d.** shaking hands

Food and Water

Circle the letter of the best answer for each question.

11. When might drinking water become unsafe?

a. during a drought

b. after a water treatment plant floods

c. before a water main breaks

d. when you are sick

12. What is one way to protect food from bacteria?

a. cook it a little

b. put it in a refrigerator

c. leave it at room temperature

d. put it on a dirty counter

Name ______________________ Class ______________ Date ______________

PUTTING PATHOGENS IN THEIR PLACE

Read the words in the box. Read the sentences. Fill in each blank with the word or phrase that best completes the sentence.

pasteurization	water
infection	wine

13. Before the twentieth century, surgery patients often died of

______________________.

14. Today, hospitals use ultraviolet radiation, boiling

______________________, and chemicals to stop infections.

15. Louis Pasteur found a way to keep ______________________ from spoiling.

16. The process named after Louis Pasteur is called

______________________.

Vaccines and Immunity

Read the words in the box. Read the sentences. Fill in each blank with the word or phrase that best completes the sentence.

antibiotic	immunity	viruses
vaccine	cowpox	

17. People who can fight disease better than others have

______________________.

18. People could fight smallpox better if they had

______________________ first.

19. A person could get immunity from a(n)

______________________.

20. You might take a(n) ______________________ to get better after a bacterial infection.

21. Antibiotics cannot kill ______________________.

Name ______________________________ Class ________________ Date ______________

Skills Worksheet

Directed Reading B

Section: Your Body's Defenses

FIRST LINES OF DEFENSE

Circle the letter of the best answer for each question.

1. What is one first line of defense in your body?

a. darkness

b. mucus

c. noise

d. warmth

2. What happens to many pathogens that enter your mouth?

a. Food destroys them.

b. Your teeth chew them.

c. Your tongue smashes them.

d. Enzymes destroy them.

3. Why can't most pathogens infect your skin?

a. Skin has layers of dead cells.

b. Skin has immunity.

c. Skin has antigens.

d. Skin is too thick.

4. How does oil on your skin help protect you?

a. It feeds the pathogens.

b. It kills pathogens.

c. It makes pathogens slip off.

d. It helps skin fall off.

FAILURE OF FIRST LINES

<u>Circle the letter</u> of the best answer for each question.

5. Which of the following help to seal an open wound?

a. antibodies

b. bacteria

c. platelets

d. veins

6. The immune system is

a. controlled by one organ.

b. controlled by two organs.

c. a team of individual cells, tissues, and organs.

d. a team of anitgens and pathogens.

CELLS OF THE IMMUNE SYSTEM

Read the description. Then, <u>draw a line</u> from the dot next to each description to the matching word.

7. proteins made by B cells	●	**a.** B cells
8. cells that destroy infected cells	●	**b.** macrophages
9. cells that engulf and digest pathogens	●	**c.** antibodies
10. cells that make antibodies	●	**d.** T cells

RESPONDING TO A VIRUS

Read the words in the box. Read the sentences. Fill in each blank with the word or phrase that best completes the sentence.

B cells	infected
killer T cells	antigens

11. When a virus gets into the body, some body cells are

______________________________.

12. Viral particles, macrophages, and infected cells are all covered with viral ______________________________.

13. Helper T cells call ______________________________ to create antibodies.

14. Helper T cells get ______________________________ to destroy infected cells.

FEVERS

fever	brain	pathogens

15. Helper T cells send a signal to your ______________________________ for your temperature to rise.

16. A fever slows the growth of some ______________________________.

17. A mild ______________________________ can help a person get well faster.

MEMORY CELLS

Circle the letter of the best answer for each question.

18. Why does your body fight infection better the second time?

a. B cells need less time to make antibodies.

b. Antibodies work better over time.

c. B cells don't exist the first time

d. Helper T cells don't call B cells the first time.

19. What kind of cells remember old infections?

a. antigens

b. killer T cells

c. helper T cells

d. memory B cells

CHALLENGES TO THE IMMUNE SYSTEM

Allergies

20. What do we call the immune system fighting something that's not dangerous?

a. an allergy

b. a disease

c. an antigen

d. an antibiotic

21. Why can't allergies be cured?

a. Allergies are deadly.

b. Allergies are not understood.

c. Doctors ignore allergies.

d. People hide allergies.

Autoimmune Diseases

22. What do we call an immune system attack?

a. a pathogen

b. an allergy

c. an antigen

d. an autoimmune disease

Circle the letter of the best answer for each question.

23. What are two examples of autoimmune diseases?

a. cancer and asthma

b. flu and mumps

c. strep throat and measles

d. Type 1 diabetes and rheumatoid arthritis

Cancer

24. In what disease do cells divide too fast?

a. AIDS

b. cancer

c. arthritis

d. lupus

25. What is the goal of cancer treatments?

a. to remove, kill, or slow the growth of cancer cells

b. to make more helper cells

c. to make cells divide faster

d. to create more antigens

AIDS

26. What does AIDS stand for?

a. Auto Immune Deficiency System

b. Actual Immunity Debt Syndrome

c. Acquired Immune Deficiency Syndrome

d. All Infections Disease System

27. What causes AIDS?

a. allergies

b. poor diet

c. HIV

d. cancer

28. What part of the body does AIDS attack?

a. the stomach

b. the immune system

c. the lungs

d. the intestines

Name ______________________ Class ______________ Date ______________

Assessment

Chapter Test C

Body Defenses and Disease

MULTIPLE CHOICE

Circle the letter of the best answer for each question.

1. What is one way people get noninfectious diseases?
   - **a.** dirty hands
   - **b.** a genetic disorder
   - **c.** being around sick people
   - **d.** being sneezed on

2. What causes infectious diseases?
   - **a.** a genetic disorder
   - **b.** heredity
   - **c.** pathogens
   - **d.** smoking

3. What is mucous?
   - **a.** a first line of defense
   - **b.** a pathogen
   - **c.** a helper cell
   - **d.** an antigen

4. What do platelets do?
   - **a.** seal open wounds
   - **b.** attack viruses
   - **c.** cause wounds
   - **d.** cure diseases

5. What is the system that attacks pathogens called?
   - **a.** antibiotic system
   - **b.** attack system
   - **c.** vaccine system
   - **d.** immune system

MULTIPLE CHOICE

Circle the letter of the best answer for each question.

6. Sometimes the immune system tries to fight antigens that are not bad. What is this called?

a. an allergy

b. a disease

c. an antigen

d. an antibiotic

7. What kind of disease is rheumatoid arthritis?

a. infectious

b. viral

c. AIDS

d. autoimmune

8. What is the disease where cells divide too fast?

a. AIDS

b. cancer

c. arthritis

d. lupus

9. What may HIV cause?

a. flu

b. strep throat

c. AIDS

d. mumps

10. What does AIDS infect?

a. the immune system

b. the heart

c. the lungs

d. the intestines

MATCHING

Read the description. Then draw a line from the dot next to each description to the matching word.

11. engulf viruses	●	**a.** sneezes
12. destroy infected cells	●	**b.** antibodies
13. send pathogens through the air	●	**c.** killer T cells
14. attach to antigens	●	**d.** macrophages

15. call other cells to fight disease	●	**a.** vaccines
16. cannot be killed by antibiotics	●	**b.** viruses
17. help people resist disease	●	**c.** helper T cells
18. split to make antibodies	●	**d.** B cells

FILL-IN-THE-BLANK

Read the words in the box. Read the sentences. Fill in each blank with the word or phrase that best completes the sentence.

immune system	infection
immunity	T cells

19. A low fever helps ______________________ and B cells to grow faster.

20. Your ______________________ can fight a disease better the second time.

21. When people have ______________________, they do not get a disease that others get.

22. Before the 20th century, surgery patients often died of ______________________.

Name ______________________ Class ______________ Date ______________

Skills Worksheet

Directed Reading B

Section: Good Nutrition

Circle the letter of the best answer for each question.

1. What does food have that helps you stay healthy?

a. nutrients

b. taste

c. flavor

d. ingredients

NUTRIENTS

2. How many kinds of nutrients does your body need?

a. 2

b. 4

c. 6

d. 8

Carbohydrates

3. Which of the following statements is NOT true of carbohydrates?

a. Carbohydrates are composed of simple sugars.

b. Carbohydrates give you energy.

c. Carbohydrates are sources of fiber.

d. Carbohydrates contain amino acids.

Read the description. Then draw a line from the dot next to each description to the matching word.

4. give you long-lasting energy	●	**a.** simple carbohydrates
5. give you quick energy	●	**b.** complex carbohydrates

Protein

<u>Circle the letter</u> of the best answer for each question.

6. What kind of nutrients help repair your body?

a. fats
b. proteins
c. carbohydrates
d. minerals

7. What are the building blocks of proteins?

a. amino acids
b. sugar
c. Calories
d. fats

Fats

Read the description. Then <u>draw a line</u> from the dot next to each description to the matching word.

8. a fat-like substance found naturally in the body •

9. kind of fat that raises cholesterol •

10. kind of fat that lowers cholesterol •

a. saturated fat

b. cholesterol

c. unsaturated fat

Water

<u>Circle the letter</u> of the best answer for each question.

11. What nutrient makes up 70% of your body?

a. water
b. proteins
c. carbohydrates
d. minerals

12. According to some scientists, how many glasses of water should you drink in a day?

a. 2
b. 4
c. 6
d. 8

Minerals

Circle the letter of the best answer for each question.

13. What are minerals?

a. elements

b. proteins

c. vitamins

d. fats

14. Why does your body need minerals?

a. to lose weight

b. to keep working right

c. to make proteins

d. to make cholesterol

Vitamins

15. Why does your body need vitamins?

a. to make cholesterol

b. to make proteins

c. to stay healthy and grow

d. to sleep better

16. What does vitamin C do?

a. protects red blood cells

b. helps the body fight disease

c. helps blood clot

d. helps keep skin healthy

Circle the letter of the best answer for each question.

17. What does vitamin E do?

a. protects red blood cells

b. helps the body fight disease

c. helps blood clot

d. helps build strong teeth

18. What does vitamin K do?

a. protects red blood cells

b. helps the body fight disease

c. helps blood clot

d. helps keep skin healthy

19. What does vitamin A do?

a. protects red blood cells

b. helps the body fight disease

c. helps blood clot

d. helps keep skin healthy

EATING FOR GOOD HEALTH

20. How can you use the Food Guide Pyramid?

a. to make healthy food choices

b. to count Calories

c. to explain food labels

d. to compare nutrients

Read the description. Then <u>draw a line</u> from the dot next to each description to the matching word.

21. Eat 3 to 5 servings each day.	●	**a.** fats, oils, and sweets
22. Eat 2 to 4 servings each day.	●	**b.** vegetables
23. Eat sparingly.	●	**c.** fruits
24. Eat 6 to 11 servings each day.	●	**d.** breads, cereals, rice, and pasta

READING FOOD LABELS

<u>Circle the letter</u> of the best answer for each question.

25. What do Nutrition Facts labels tell you about food?

a. how many nutrients are in one serving

b. how much to eat

c. where to buy food

d. how to cook food

NUTRITIONAL DISORDERS

26. What causes nutritional disorders?

a. bad teeth

b. bad hygiene

c. bad eating habits

d. too many minerals

27. What is malnutrition?

a. not getting enough nutrients

b. having too much body fat

c. eating too many fruits

d. counting Calories

Anorexia Nervosa and Bulimia Nervosa

Circle the letter of the best answer for each question.

28. What is anorexia nervosa?

a. getting enough nutrients

b. having too much body fat

c. binge eating and forcing yourself to throw up

d. starving yourself

29. What is bulimia nervosa?

a. getting enough nutrients

b. having too much body fat

c. binge eating and forcing yourself to throw up

d. starving yourself

Obesity

30. What is obesity?

a. not getting enough nutrients

b. having too much body fat

c. binge eating and forcing yourself to throw up

d. starving yourself

Name ______________________ Class ______________ Date ____________

Skills Worksheet

Directed Reading B

Section: Risks of Alcohol and Other Drugs

WHAT IS A DRUG?

Circle the letter of the best answer for each question.

1. What is a substance that causes changes in your body or mind called?

a. an addiction

b. a craving

c. an element

d. a drug

Read the description. Then draw a line from the dot next to each description to the matching word.

2. drugs that speed up the nervous system ●

3. drugs that control symptoms of colds and allergies ●

4. drugs that fight bacterial infections ●

5. drugs that slow the nervous system ●

6. drugs that relieve pain ●

a. antihistamines

b. depressants

c. stimulants

d. antibiotics

e. analgesics

DEPENDENCE AND ADDICTION

Read the words in the box. Read the sentences. Fill in each blank with the word or phrase that best completes the sentence.

tolerance	addiction	physical dependence
psychological dependence		withdrawal symptoms

7. When a drug user needs more and more of a drug, he or she has a(n) ______________________ to the drug.

8. When a drug abuser's body needs a drug, he or she has a(n) ______________________.

9. A drug abuser who needs a drug and does not get it may then have ______________________.

10. If a person cannot control drug use, he or she has a(n) ______________________.

11. When people feel cravings for a drug, it is called ______________________.

TYPES OF DRUGS

Herbal Medicines

Circle the letter of the best answer for each question.

12. Why should herbs be used carefully?

a. They help you sleep.

b. They do not affect the body the way drugs do.

c. They are not guaranteed safe by the Federal Drug Administration.

d. They do not help you heal.

Over-the-Counter and Prescription Drugs

Read the words in the box. Read the sentences. Fill in each blank with the word or phrase that best completes the sentence.

prescription	over-the-counter drugs	side effects

13. Drugs that you don't need a prescription to buy are called

______________________________.

14. A doctor must write a(n) ______________________________

for you to buy some drugs.

15. Sometimes, a drug has uncomfortable symptoms, which are called

______________________________.

Circle the letter of the best answer for each question.

16. Which of these is a drug safety tip?

- **a.** It is okay to share drugs.
- **b.** Read the label before you take a drug.
- **c.** If you don't feel better, take more drugs.
- **d.** Don't ask your doctor how to take drugs.

17. Which of these is NOT a drug safety tip?

- **a.** Throw out leftover drugs.
- **b.** Read the label before you take a drug.
- **c.** It is okay to share drugs.
- **d.** Ask your doctor how to take drugs.

Tobacco

Circle the letter of the best answer for each question.

18. What do cigarettes have that is addictive?

a. ashes

b. nicotine

c. paper

d. smoke

19. What disease is often caused by smoking?

a. lung cancer

b. obesity

c. anorexia nervosa

d. bulimia nervosa

20. What kind of cancer can smokeless tobacco often cause?

a. mouth cancer

b. lung cancer

c. nose cancer

d. ear cancer

Alcohol

21. Which of the following is NOT true about alcoholism?

a. Alcoholism is considered a disease.

b. Alcoholism is a dependency on nicotine.

c. Alcoholism may be caused by genetic factors.

d. Alcoholism is dependency on alcohol.

Marijuana

<u>Circle the letter</u> of the best answer for each question.

22. Which of the following does marijuana NOT cause?

a. slow reaction time

b. impaired thinking

c. feelings of anxiety

d. intense excitement

Cocaine

23. Cocaine produces what kind of feeling?

a. excitement

b. hatred

c. paranoia

d. sleepiness

Narcotics and Designer Drugs

24. What kind of drug is made from the opium plant?

a. alcohol

b. narcotic

c. marijuana

d. cocaine

25. What kind of drugs are made by making small changes to existing drugs?

a. prescription drugs

b. narcotics

c. designer drugs

d. antidepressants

Hallucinogens

Circle the letter of the best answer for each question.

26. What does NOT happen when you take hallucinogens?

a. mood changes

b. distorted senses

c. brain damage

d. nicotine withdrawal

DRUG ABUSE

How Drug Abuse Starts

27. Which of these is NOT true about drugs?

a. It can be hard to quit taking drugs.

b. Cigarettes are not addictive.

c. Some people use drugs to make friends.

d. Alcohol abuse is as bad as drug abuse.

28. Why do many people start taking illegal drugs?

a. Friends ask them to do it.

b. Parents say it is okay.

c. Doctors tell them to do it.

d. Schools supply drugs.

Getting Off Drugs

29. What can make it hard to quit drugs?

a. support from family

b. withdrawal symptoms

c. drug treatment centers

d. wanting to quit

Name ______________________ Class ______________ Date ____________

Skills Worksheet

Directed Reading B

Section: Healthy Habits

TAKING CARE OF YOUR BODY

Circle the letter of the best answer for each question.

1. What is the science of protecting your health called?

a. aerobics

b. hygiene

c. healthiness

d. washing

2. What is the best way to avoid getting sick?

a. using sunscreen

b. washing your hair

c. brushing your teeth

d. washing your hands

Good Posture

3. What can you imagine to help you have good posture?

a. a box around your head

b. a line down your body

c. a square behind your feet

d. a circle around your body

Exercise

4. What does aerobic exercise do for you?

a. increases heart rate

b. makes you slow down

c. makes you hungry

d. increases intake of Calories

Circle the letter of the best answer for each question.

5. What is constant exercise that lasts 20 minutes or more called?

a. aerobic exercise

b. strength exercise

c. regular exercise

d. daily exercise

6. Which of these is NOT an aerobic exercise?

a. swimming

b. riding a bike

c. sitting

d. running

Sleep

7. How much sleep should a teenager get each night?

a. 12 hours

b. 9.5 hours

c. 8 hours

d. 4 hours

COPING WITH STRESS

8. What is stress?

a. a response to pressure

b. a low grade

c. anger

d. a response to exercise

Circle the letter of the best answer for each question.

9. Which of these is NOT a sign of stress?

a. getting upset

b. being relaxed

c. having a headache

d. having trouble sleeping

Dealing with Stress

10. Which of these is NOT a good way to handle stress?

a. sharing problems

b. exercising regularly

c. getting angry

d. relaxing

INJURY PREVENTION

11. Why should accidents be avoided?

a. Accidents are messy.

b. Accidents can cause injury or death.

c. Accidents cost money.

d. Accidents take a lot of time.

Safety Outdoors

Read the description. Then draw a line from the dot next to each description to the matching word.

12. purifying the drinking water	●	**a.** camping safety
13. wearing a life jacket	●	**b.** swimming safety
14. never swimming alone	●	**c.** boating safety

Safety at Home

Circle the letter of the best answer for each question.

15. Where should smoke detectors be installed?

a. in every room

b. on every floor

c. in the kitchen only

d. in the basement only

Read the description. Then, draw a line from the dot next to each description to the matching part of the picture.

16. a good place for nonslip mats ●

17. a bad place to leave items lying around ●

18. a good place to clean up spills quickly ●

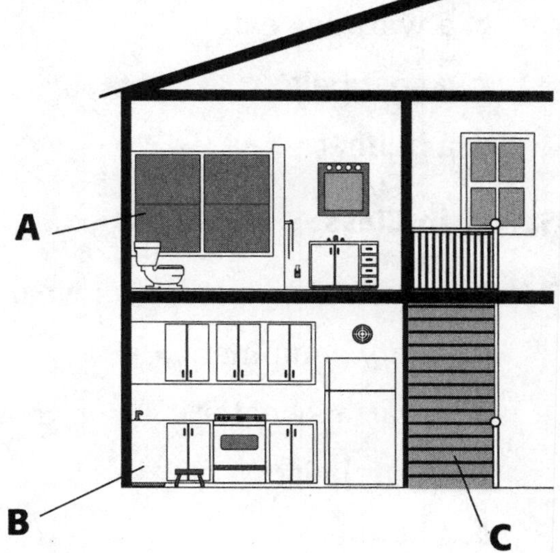

Safety on the Road

Circle the letter of the best answer for each question.

19. What should you always wear in the car?

a. a pair of gloves

b. a warm sweater

c. a seat belt

d. a helmet

20. What should you always wear on a bike?

a. a pair of gloves

b. a warm sweater

c. a seat belt

d. a helmet

Safety in Class

21. What should you always wear in a lab or wood shop?

a. safety equipment

b. a warm sweater

c. a seat belt

d. a helmet

22. Whose instructions should you follow while in lab class or woodworking class?

a. no one's instructions

b. your friends' instructions

c. the teacher's instructions

d. other students' instructions

WHEN ACCIDENTS HAPPEN

Circle the letter of the best answer for each question.

23. What is the first thing you should do if you see an accident happen?

a. check for other dangers

b. run away

c. try first aid

d. ask what happened

Call for Help

24. In most communities, what number can you call for help?

a. 711

b. 411

c. 911

d. 611

Learn First Aid

25. What can you do to learn how to help injured people?

a. take a first-aid class

b. study nutrition

c. ask your friends

d. call 911

Name ________________ Class ________ Date ________

Assessment

Chapter Test C

Staying Healthy

MULTIPLE CHOICE

Circle the letter of the best answer for each question.

1. What is the body's main source of energy?

a. minerals

b. vitamins

c. carbohydrates

d. water

2. What is one of the best ways to keep from getting sick?

a. staying home

b. taking medicine

c. taking a nap

d. washing your hands

3. What drugs fight bacterial infection?

a. antibiotics

b. antihistamines

c. analgesics

d. narcotics

4. What drugs help with pain?

a. antibiotics

b. depressants

c. analgesics

d. nicotine

Circle the letter of the best answer for each question.

5. What drugs help with cold symptoms?

a. hallucinogens

b. antihistamines

c. analgesics

d. narcotics

6. What can you learn that will help injured people?

a. hygiene

b. first aid

c. tolerance

d. stress relief

7. Where might you go for help with a drug abuse problem?

a. a drug treatment center

b. the place you bought the drug

c. a safety center

d. a nutrition center

8. What should you always wear when riding a bike?

a. a seat belt

b. a helmet

c. gloves

d. a hat

9. What should you always wear when riding in a car?

a. a seat belt

b. a helmet

c. gloves

d. a hat

10. What should you always use when working in a lab class?

a. a seat belt

b. a helmet

c. a scarf

d. safety equipment

MATCHING

Read the description. Then, draw a line from the dot next to each description to the matching word.

11. helps you have a stronger heart ●
12. helps protect red blood cells ●
13. helps warn of a fire ●
14. helps you keep good health ●

a. vitamin E
b. aerobic exercise
c. good hygiene
d. smoke detector

---

15. a disease linked to alcohol ●
16. a disease linked to smoking ●
17. loss of control over drug use ●
18. not getting enough nutrients ●

a. lung cancer
b. alcoholism
c. addiction
d. malnutrition

FILL-IN-THE-BLANK

Read the words in the box. Read the sentences. Fill in each blank with the word or phrase that best completes the sentence.

anorexia nervosa	obesity
cholesterol	carbohydrate

19. A fat-like substance found naturally in the body is called

______________________.

20. The kind of nutrient that gives you energy is a(n)

______________________.

21. An illness where a person does not eat enough is called

______________________.

22. A high percentage of body fat is a sign of

______________________.